& GRACE

& Grace

Selections from
Lexington Poetry Month 2015

Edited By
Christopher McCurry

Accents Publishing • Lexington, Kentucky • 2016

Copyright © 2016 by Accents Publishing
All rights reserved

Printed in the United States of America

Accents Publishing
Editors: Christopher McCurry
Cover Image: *Balancing Act* by Audrey Rooney

Library of Congress Control Number: 2016937141
ISBN: 978-1-936628-42-1
First Edition

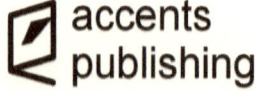

Accents Publishing is an independent press for brilliant voices. For a catalog of current and upcoming titles, please visit us on the Web at

www.accents-publishing.com

CONTENTS

Introduction / xi

This I Pray

ARE YOU GOING TO HEAVEN? / *Jim Lally* / 3
WRITING &C / *Hap Houlihan* / 4
SOMEONE ASKS IF I'M AN ATHEIST / *Madison Miller* / 5
FATHER I WANT TO BE / *Patrick Maloney* / 7
ON DELEGATING TASKS / *Delmar Reffett* / 8
TOO LONG AWAY / *Kari Burchfield* / 9
SOUVENIR / *Matthew Haughton* / 10
FIRST LIGHTNING BUG SIGHTING, 2015 / *Rona Roberts* / 11
MOONSHINE TASTING / *Laurel Dixon* / 12
SLEEP THE PAIN AWAY / *LaTosha Pence* / 13
FOURTEEN—A TAOIST PARABLE / *carole johnston* / 14
SMALL STONE #28 / *Mary Dusing* / 15
IS IT I, LORD? / *Jennifer Standard* / 16
SEARCH ENGINE LIMIT / *George Ella Lyon* / 17
JOAN OF ARC / *EllePiggy* / 18
SOMEWHERE IN SOUTH CAROLINA, … / *JD Lester* / 19
SCORCHING / *Kendrick VanZant* / 23
PRAISE SONG FOR THE LAG / *Katerina Stoykova-Klemer* / 24
WHAT I THINK WHEN YOU ARE THE … / *Eduardo Ballestero* / 25
FORTUNE TELLER / *Maya Pemble* / 26
SALVATION / *Sofiah Sexton* / 27
MAKE MY MARK / *Terre Brothers Johnson* / 28
TO THE SUICIDE BOMBER AT KARNAK / *Chloe Forsting* / 29
NARCISSISTIC MINIMALIST / *JW Mullins* / 30
IRIDESCENT, ANCIENT, AND CRUMBLING / *Jessica Swafford* / 31
QUESTIONNAIRE / *Robert Campbell* / 32
LAST ACT OF KINDNESS / *Dennis Preston* / 33

In the Name Of

LAWLESS / *Misty Skaggs* / 37
SYCAMORE / *Kristy Robinson Horine* / 38
ENTROPY / *Julian DeVille* / 40

WRECK: A NOUN / *Jeremy Paden* / 41
MY COMPANION 1994 – 2008 / *Linda Caldwell* / 43
RED BUD / *Barbara Sabol* / 44
THIRST / *Jay McCoy* / 45
MAY ALLURE / *Michayla Gatsos* / 46
WET FEET / *T.D. Worthington* / 47
MADRIGAL / *Sherry Chandler* / 48
ON THE HILL ABOVE THE RIVER, ... / *Unwit* / 49
SEQUOIADENDRON GIGANTEUM / *Beatrice Underwood-Sweet* / 50
FOUND PARADOX / *Mary L Allen* / 51
BRAD PITT STANDS IN A STORM / *Rain E. Palmer* / 52
CONTRA. / *Hannah Bishop* / 53
BELTED KINGFISHER / *Amy Camuglia* / 54
THE COYOTE / *Erin Chandler* / 55
SHIVA, HER STATUE / *Bernard Deville* / 56
MY BODY // MY WARZONE: FINGERS / *Allie Marini* / 57
A NEW HAIR CUT / *Heather Dent* / 58
THE CLIENT / *c.l. kirby* / 60
HYPERLEXIA / *M J Eaton* / 61
MORNING WALK / *Rudy Thomas* / 62
TO LIZ ON THE ROAD / *B.David Perry* / 63
CRICKET / *Joshua Moore* / 64
OBSCENITIES #2, #3, #4 / *Jiv Johnson* / 65
HEADLINES AND A DREAM (ZUIHITSU) / *Douglas E. Self* / 67
ELEVATOR CONVERSATION / *Joseph Camuglia* / 69
SHI-I-N: THE SOUND OF NOTHING / *Chuck Clenney* / 70

The Father

THE MATERNITY WARD / *Serena Devi* / 73
I WANT TO BUILD / *Andrew Depew* / 74
THE INVISIBLE MAN AT THE GROCER / *Robert S. King* / 75
LUCIFEROUS / *Joseph Allen Nichols* / 76
AT THE COMPANY PICNIC / *Don Boes* / 78
ONCE, WHEN I WAS YOUR MOTHER / *Liz Prather* / 79
THE GREAT GREY / *Jude Lally* / 80
INSIDE A FRAGILE BODY / *Pat Owen* / 81
THINKING OF ABRAHAM / *Jonel Sallee* / 82
HE WANTS A HANGOVER / *Bronson O'Quinn* / 83
MY MOTHER WRITES ABOUT ... / *Pauletta Hansel* / 84

A WOMAN'S SHEPHERD / *Elizabeth Beck* / *85*
PAINTED NAILS PROVE / *Lucia Cherciu* / *86*
THE BRAIN IS NOT THE MIND / *Alx Johns* / *87*
CALL IT DESTINY / *Katrin Flores* / *88*
IT ALL ADDS UP / *Tina Parker* / *89*
YOU = TIME MACHINE / *Lennart Lundh* / *90*
DAD TELLS US WE ARE RAISING ... / *Melva Sue Priddy* / *91*
WHAT MY FATHER FELT / *ashley parker owens* / *92*
SCARLET RIBBONS / *K. Bruce Florence* / *93*
WHY I AM RETICENT / *J. Wise* / *95*
ALL THE NIGHT STARS / *Linda Caldwell* / *96*
DAY 25 / *Lynnell Edwards* / *97*
IN MOTION / *Jeffrey Helton* / *98*
ASK AND YE SHALL / *Luke Wallin* / *99*
CHILDREN OF ABRAHAM DEBATE ... / *Bobby Steve Baker* / *100*
MURDER MY MACHISMO / *Alex Simand* / *101*

The Son

GO / *Jennifer Barricklow* / *105*
GABE: A REQUEST OF YOUR PRESENCE / *Rae Cobbs* / *106*
DEAD ARTIST'S DAUGHTER / *Erin Mathews* / *108*
DAUGHTER / *Christopher McCurry* / *109*
OVERLY CONCERNED / *hb elam* / *110*
LITTLE A / *Joan Burke* / *113*
SOFT / *Stevie Farmer* / *114*
I STARE / *Christopher Miller* / *115*
THE CHANGELING REFLECTS ON ... / *Elizabeth Burton* / *118*
BAIT SHOP / *Duke Gatsos* / *120*
BROTHER / *Jennifer Beckett* / *121*
THE GRADUATE / *Brittany Castle* / *122*
WHERE THE WALL MEETS THE FLOOR / *Sean L Corbin* / *123*
LONG OFF WET BELL / *Colin Boyd* / *124*
ALL NIGHT LONG / *Sue Neufarth Howard* / *125*
TOO HAPPY SO I, / *J. L. Taylor* / *126*
HAT TRICK DIADEM / *meadowdawn* / *128*
HARD YEAR / *Maggie Brewer* / *129*
FILLER / *Randall Walden* / *131*
PATCHWORK WOMAN / *Bianca Lynne Spriggs* / *132*
WORLD CUP STRATEGY FOR ... / *Gaby Bedetti* / *134*

THE GOOD OF THE GRAPE / *Karlee Caswell* / 135
BEFORE THIS / *Jason Lee Miller* / 136
15.6.30 / *GA Smith* / 138
ALIX DREAMS OF AN END, BUT NOT THE END / *Victoria Sullivan* / 139
ON A HEARING IN CHARLESTON / *Dorothy Bouzouma* / 140

& The Holy Ghost

"OF COURSE THERE'S AN AFTERLIFE" / *Sarah Freligh* / 147
IN THE DIP BEYOND ... / *Poetessa Leixyl Kaye Emmerson* / 148
CONSTELLATION / *Jonathon La Mar* / 149
FIVE DIRECTIONS TO MY HOUSE / *Karen George* / 150
OUR TIME / *Vijay Singh* / 151
BELIEVING / *Amanda Kelley* / 152
I SLEEP LIKE THE #4 / *Debbie Adams Cooper* / 153
WE SLEEP ON PAPER / *Michelle Knickerbocker* / 154
POET IN THE CORNER / *Holly Wooten* / 155
FIRE / *Alexis* / 157
LIFE IN A TEA CUP / *Tara Cremeans-Mounger* / 158
SESTINA & I / *Aidan Ziliak* / 159
HOW WE LIVE LOVE / *Harriet Windsor* / 161
I WILL HEM THE SKIRT OF YOUR PAIN / *Savannah Sipple* / 162
THIS MORNING, I LAUGH / *Elizabeth Sands Wise* / 163
I SAW THE *FRANK* IN *HANK* AND ... / *Nettie Farris* / 164
BAD SEX / *MC DK* / 165
TRUE LOVE / *Valerie L. Wells* / 166
It's impossible, this love of ours: / *Zlatna Kostova* / 167
AFTER / *Jude McPherson* / 168
AFTER PRIDE / *K. Nicole Wilson* / 169
JUST BEFORE / *Whitney Baker* / 170
YESTERDAY / *Jordan Quinn* / 171
TO THE GUY WHO ATE ALL MY ... / *Allison Thorpe* / 172
CRAIG'S LIST: MISSED CONNECTION / *Keith Stewart* / 174
THINGS WITH ME AND SPIDERS 2. NOCTURNE / *Bianca Bargo* / 175
FOGGED / *Cleo* / 177
BEING ALONE / *Amanda Holt* / 178
RUNNING / *Abigail Caldwell-Gatsos* / 179
GEORGIA AQUARIUM BELUGA WHALE ... / *Leigh Anne Hornfeldt* / 180
WHAT I'LL WRITE ABOUT IF I EVER ... / *Jason Williams* / 181

FACING IT / *Nora Burton / 182*
SEVEN CIRCLES / *Sue Churchill / 183*

The Poets / 187

About the Editor / 203

Sponsors / 204

INTRODUCTION

As I was trying to think about what to say to introduce this anthology, how I selected these poems, how the section titles came about, I did what any writer facing a difficult problem does: I logged onto my Facebook account. While scrolling through the newsfeed, I came across this status update by fellow Lexington Poetry Month poet, Whitney Baker:

> My need to what I call pray exceeds my need to understand what I am doing or to whom or what my action is directed.

The only formal prayer I was ever able to memorize was the *Our Father*. (I grew up Catholic, sort of.) It resonated with me as a child and still does. Despite being distant from religion these days, that prayer, much like the poems selected to represent Lexington Poetry Month 2015, expresses to me a need to call out to someone, something, greater than our individual selves. In recognizing that need, we give into the lack of understanding, the hope and the doubt that whatever *it* is, it could be listening: it might hear us. That, to me, is human. It is poetry.

The poems collected here do not seek to define or codify, include or exclude. They share a desire, maybe only tonally, to be heard. Through this, the collective voice of one hundred and forty one poets emerges. If I may, I'd like to suggest that by sharing these poems with one another, through the Accents Publishing blog, we are doing something inexplicable, and by responding to one another, we are doing something holy.

I know this sounds hyperbolic and sentimental, but spend some time with these poems, read them out loud; it will feel like praying.

—*Christopher McCurry*

For a complete list of participating poets and their submissions, visit
accents-publishing.com/blog/lexpomo2015/2015-poets/

This I Pray

ARE YOU GOING TO HEAVEN?
by Jim Lally

are you going to heaven?
someone on the radio asks

flies in the kitchen
and on the table
an eye of needle
      —out the window
a red bird in the dead
peach tree,
      hope
like a wishbone not pulled

WRITING &C

by Hap Houlihan

lord my lord: sometimes,
it's as difficult and dangerous as
toting a stand-up bass (in a case)
up 16 flights of rusty far-escape stairs

but god my god, sometimes,
it's just as easy as looking down,
saying a little prayer to nobody,
and jumping off the top.

SOMEONE ASKS IF I'M AN ATHEIST
by Madison Miller

I reply,
"I believe in God,
when I need to."
And tonight
I'd sing hallelujah
to a God
I don't believe in.
Tonight I need to.
Tonight I need
some sort of father.
Or some sort of savior.
Or some sort of divinity
to hold me together.
Most days
I find strength
within myself.
Tonight
my eyes
are tired.
My hands
are shaking and
my feet
are sore.
I am scattered
and tattered
and frail
tonight.
Hallelujah to
any entity that
makes this easier.
Maybe it never

gets easier.
Maybe prayers
go in vain.
But tonight
I am unwilling
to be the one
sacrificing
my own flesh
for someone else's
sin.

FATHER I WANT TO BE
by Patrick Maloney

Father I want to be a weeping willow
> *No son, you will be an axe*

Father I want to be a seahorse
> *No son, you will be a great white*

Father I want to be the purple rose Mother was
> *No. You already have enough thorns*

Father I want to be a constellation asleep
on dark water
> *No son, you must be a fisherman*
> *of the stars and the sand that slipped*
> *through my fist*

ON DELEGATING TASKS
by Delmar Reffett

Was it Your curiosity,
or that placid laze of divinity,
passive as parting clouds,
leisurely as long garden walks
in the cool of the evening,
that left Adam to offer names to paradise?

Was it keeping the Sabbath
by keeping to Yourself
those earlier names
that spoke the world into being
with sinister ease inside the void?
Would anything else have broken Your day of rest?

The beasts of the field,
resentful still,
mutter their maiden names to themselves,
grazing in the dark.

The fishes of the sea
second-guess themselves;
unsure what to answer to,
they stay away from the surface when called.

The fowls of the air,
in frenzied chorus,
are alone in still trying to correct us.
They neither sow nor reap,
but gather together and continue to speak.

TOO LONG AWAY
by Kari Burchfield

I don't need
to buy another notebook
to fret about where to start
or where to end
or even what it will be about

I do need
my daughter's smile
my husband's hand
my dog's waggy tail

I don't need
forced symmetry

I rather enjoy
this adirondack chair
in one of my old favorite writing spots

I could do without
ants
and bird poop
and all the what ifs and should haves

I'm glad I
read the blog today
had lunch outside
smiled

SOUVENIR
by Matthew Haughton

I want to thank the two-winged sugar maple seed
I found this morning
for letting me keep him in my shirt pocket.
All afternoon he seemed to flutter at my breast
like a moth drawn to an open candle.
By evening he had crumbled, as if survival
had become something impossible,
disintegrated for a year until his next arrival.

FIRST LIGHTNING BUG SIGHTING, 2015
by Rona Roberts

On Wittland Street you rise to paint the night—
Lift too, my summer heart, that loves this sight.

MOONSHINE TASTING
by Laurel Dixon

Mouths full of moonshine   tasted   from plastic
communion cups   amen   to this trial by fire
palms down   on the sticky   wooden counter top

 And may we pray   with our mouths   sweet with liquor
Laura   may we pray   in 32 flavors
Like apple pie   and blackberry   and Hillbilly Punch

Or forget prayers   and live   by only this sweetness
These seven years   spun between us   the muggy night
conversation   scent of jasmine   lavender   the wink

of the moonshine   above   all our hope
spilled out   like rain   that rises   in the morning
to wash us home   clean   tired   desirous   of sleep

SLEEP THE PAIN AWAY
by LaTosha Pence

Take me to a lullaby
Another dimension if you will
Astral project to a happier place

Sleep the pain away.

Absorb the healing
Comes
In rest, with mind alert
I travel in bliss
Events surreal
I won't want to miss

Happenings in my mind
To be real
Or just perceived as such?

Regardless, it fascinates
And takes away this grief
To be or not to be?
Asleep and aboard
This train that has no bounds

FOURTEEN—A TAOIST PARABLE
by carole johnston

dreamed I was
a butterfly at midnight
enchanted

by the glittering dark
like ancient Chuang Tzu
wondering what was real

in that famous
dream Chuang Tzu became
confused

did the butterfly also dream
she was Chuang Tzu?

if I dream
I'm a butterfly

at midnight
will I forget that once
I couldn't fly?

am I the butterfly
or just a midnight dreamer
identity lost

in glamorous flight?
close my eyes and wonder

SMALL STONE #28
by Mary Dusing

> The dove startled
> from its slumber
> in the pine tree
> by the light
> flies blindly
> into the window
> again and again

IS IT I, LORD?

by Jennifer Standard

I sit in church, listening to the preacher
Is it I, Lord?
Noting he's a wonderful speaker
I sit in church, listening to the choir
Is it I, Lord?
Noting that the hymns do not lie
I sit in church, watching the ushers help people sit
Is it I, Lord?
God blessed the unity of the pulpit.
To reach the masses and preach God's word
Is it I, Lord?
So that your answer may be heard

SEARCH ENGINE LIMIT
by George Ella Lyon

You can't cure
a sore throat
by Googling
salt water.

JOAN OF ARC
by EllePiggy

black cat in my backyard
a rabbit dashes under the fence

last night i found a dead snake
limp leather on my porch like a gift—

snow peas covered in dew
the green buds of a blueberry bush

and everywhere i walk, i displace
entire peoples, crawling and skittering—

there are no wailing stones or crooked crosses
only brimming creeks and summer breath

my life is not a Murakami novel
my life is mud between the rivers of my palms—

and i am praying to a god
that might not exist

SOMEWHERE IN SOUTH CAROLINA, A SANCTUARY SPEAKS
by JD Lester

I saw him coming,
sidling up,
slick as a snake intent
on a rabbit dinner.

Just had that look about him.
He's been by before,
eying the Sunday parishioners,
passing by with his shifty
2nd Amendment swagger,
and the bulge of cold mission
proud in his pants.

Nothing I could do, of course.
My bricks have been mortared
for centuries
by coagulated tears and
mingled Hallelujahs,
by the insoluble grace of injustice
overcome,
by Scripture recited aloud
like a binding glue,
by potluck suppers,
and enough laughter to blow a hurricane right back out to sea.

My bones are shored by worship song casting off every imaginable wrong;
my skin is bound by the conviction of raised hands,
and the lifting up of souls
for deliverance,
and deliverance,

and deliverance,
amen.

But I saw him alright.
Skinny little feller,
white as a sliced biscuit,
not a drop of honey,
not a speck of sorghum in that child.

He had those terrible FOX eyes,
glazed by a flickering dull, blue light
that gives thick cataracts of hate
to a susceptible boy.

From a block away,
I could feel that anger blazing up,
burning like a white heat
in his belly,
distended on a poor diet of oily murmurs,
rancid innuendos,
and coded black lies.

Oh, yes, I saw him coming,
furtive as a basement rat.
What could I do, though,
but wait to hold spilled blood
in my piney hands,
keen those screams back from my rafters,
amplifying the horror
like real horror rightly deserves?

What could I do
but catch the fainting,

steady the grieving,
and hold the stunned?

I've seen so much inside these walls.
Long ago, I listened to
the whispered idea of freedom,
tasted inside frightened dry mouths,
and wrapped in worried prayers.
I heard the strategies of rebellion taking shape,
steeled with the fervor of men
just wanting to walk free on Creation like any other man.

Every word ever said remains buried here:
in the smooth grain of these pews,
in the crease of hymnals,
in the echo of organ pipes,
in the scuffs of a fidgety child,
hidden here and there
like long-ago Easter eggs
that were never found.
I assure you,
those words are still here,
and I know them,
every one.

And they will rise again
on different tongues
for a new day
and a different rebellion.

The book says,
love your enemies,
turn the other cheek.

But how are you supposed to do that,
when one cheek
is pressed into the new chapel carpet,
emptying a martyr's red blood -
same red as a white man's -
and the other is facing Heaven?

SCORCHING
by Kendrick VanZant

sometimes I feel like
God's dropped cigarette
forgotten to burn a hole in reality
and I keep waiting to drop through
but it just keeps going down
and the fire that scorches is my heart
and the fire will not go out unless I let it

PRAISE SONG FOR THE LAG
by Katerina Stoykova-Klemer

Praise the lag
between losing
and finding out.
Praise the time
lapse, its surgical tick-tock,
its cradle of innocence,
the peace
before the pain.
Praise its calm
quiet, praise
the womb of its
not-yet-truth. Praise
the ordinary outbreath
before the end of earth
and air. The gasp.
The pause.
The rebirth
of beginning again.

WHAT I THINK WHEN YOU ARE THE SHOULDER I LEAN ON
by Eduardo Ballestero

You are the broad trunk
of a hundred-year maple in bloom.

FORTUNE TELLER
by Maya Pemble

how will we   ferociously
    devour soft morning
caramel   my spherical moonstone
     of secrets   tells all   memories
        filmed with dust,   a teardrop
of torn grass in spring
               the splintered piano
of her fury
       is mocking my money loss
because universes   at random
       just
          imploded

SALVATION
by Sofiah Sexton

Breast sacrificed
For survival
Secrets sacrificed
For order
Expression sacrificed
For peace
Mind opened
For enlightenment
Heart opened
For love
Soul opened
For redemption

MAKE MY MARK
by Terre Brothers Johnson

Use this bone to write my name.
Etch it into the flesh of the earth (she can take it).
Let the tears of rain wash it away again,
Paying lip service to mortality.

TO THE SUICIDE BOMBER AT KARNAK
by Chloe Forsting

Did you think the stone would start crumbling
When your body was blown to pieces?

That the statues would leak corrosive tears
As the tourists jumped, a flock of startled herons?

That this threat, this mordant advertisement,
Would domino the pillars of the Great Hypostyle Hall?

That stone rams would implode, headless but unbleeding,
As the new worshippers fled from the banks of the Nile?

That a frail Amun-Re would abdicate his temple-throne
To make way for the God you have in mind?

Don't be so hasty. Don't force the inevitable.
When we are gone, Karnak will fall on its own.

NARCISSISTIC MINIMALIST
by JW Mullins

                                        me.

IRIDESCENT, ANCIENT, AND CRUMBLING
by Jessica Swafford

A lone utterance.
The figuring and sums added.
Ashy elbows—iridescent—
Ancient dragons.
The castle crumbling,
Overtaken by
Ivy, kudzu, honeysuckle.
There are no castles left
Unless you count
The pawn shop variety
Or that relic
On Versailles Rd.
It's the realization
Of failed dreams.
No knights left—
Barely any brave souls.
Things once certain
And felt in the blood—
GONE.
Everyone quaivers,
Prickly and precarious
Have become
The new order.

QUESTIONNAIRE
by Robert Campbell

Tell us what twists your colon into knots.
Do you endeavor to tone your tummy?
Does your triple chin get up to trouble?

How well do you embrace wellness, on a scale
of one to negative eight? Where does the true
you dwell? Have you heard strange noises

in bed at night? Fill in the blank. Do you rise
to find hand prints on your ribs, your back,
the impression of a fist pushing out of your

love handles? Multiple choice now. What
can you do to unleash the really real you?
What will it look like, reader, emerging

from the slack cocoon of you, flinging you off
like a rubber sheet? Circle only one. Where
will it prowl in its wildness, self-improver, once

freed from your stifling sleeve? Can you
let go, loser, of that which holds you back?
Complete this sentence: I long to excise

my [blank]. Do you dote upon your thin
inner creature? True or false. Have you fed it
raw gall bladder? Do you routinely swallow

the treats it craves on cheat days: bone meal,
painkillers, cocaine? Can you fit a red hot
cleaver into your fat maw? Truth or dare.

When will you learn to suck back your beer gut,
your incredulity towards us, the ones who want
to help you, the ones you are dying to meet?

LAST ACT OF KINDNESS
by Dennis Preston

from her hospital room
I look out
into the hallway
someone has wheeled
a cart with drinks
and snacks
outside
the room
next door
I know what this means
one gets to go home
one does not

In the Name Of

LAWLESS
by Misty Skaggs

I try to tell
my friends from town—
there ain't no law on the Ridge.
No blue lights flashing in your mirrors
no po-po on patrol.
Just one, wore-out state boy
with three counties to cover
and no overtime pay in sight.
You don't have to worry

about how big your bonfire gets
or how loudly your music echoes
off the foothills
and the woods.
The neighbors won't call the cops
because there ain't no neighbors
and there ain't no cops
and the sheriff can't be bothered
to gas up the cruiser
more than once a week.

SYCAMORE
by Kristy Robinson Horine

And here, there was a
slow, gentle swallowing.

She had pushed her feet
into the soil,
stretched her arms
tall and wide into the sky,
dressed wisely for each season,
and let the white parts show
like she was supposed to.

And then they came
    —all five—
they came.

And they climbed her smooth body,
and they pushed off her knees, elbows,
and they leaned into her ample arms,
and they peeled back her skin,
and they carved their names within her breast,
in the order of their birth:

Hermon Clayton
Barry Melvin
Thomas Grant
William Charles
Daniel Stuart

(As if they had licked their fingers and touched the top crust and
    declared Mine, Mine, Mine!)
Brave Baroness of the bottomland

with her slow, gentle swallowing
of the heirs who were bequeathed
        this—
            the Sycamore.

ENTROPY
by Julian DeVille

what if god's a state of mind?
Pride fucking with you,
building a recursion fortress
for your curiosity to live out
its days in luxury?
what if there exists coincidence?
Holy moments of sheer luck the
defining points of our show,
replayed for discussion at
poetry readings, some
earning timelessness
and a little money?
what if it's all chaotic?
calculated yet ambiguous
like a pendulum without gravity
carving paths through entropy,
the less likely an event, the
more meaningful it becomes.

WRECK: A NOUN
by Jeremy Paden

wreck: noun, early 13th century, from the Anglo-French which took it from the Old Norse *rek,* related to *reka* which means *to drive* or *push* (not in the sense of controlling a motor vehicle, but urging a herd of animals forward & later the force of waves & currents washing debris up onto the shore), related to the Proto-Germanic *wreken,* now *wreak,* which used to mean *to mete out vengeance* & also *to pursue,* even *prosecute* & these (*wreck* & *wreak*) are all confused in Middle & early modern English with *wrack,* as in wrack & ruin, & *rack,* as in the wooden torture frame (so similar to the gurney I spent that first night on, under lights that never dimmed), & *wretch,* as in a person lost in suffering, one wracked & rent asunder, even cast out of the city.

1—as a noun it first meant the destruction of a ship at sea, then the destruction of any vehicle or building brought to ruin. as in: when your car ran the light & mangled the front end of my car & bent its metal rack, both were wrecks—as was the car you hit after mine, before the light post you knocked into the building & stopped your forward movement.

2—(legal) those goods washed ashore, or that flotsam fished from the sea, & claimed by no one. as in: that book on beauty's relationship to justice I was reading & the Townes Van Zandt CD left in the ruined car, but not my wretched body wracked with pain on the gurney watched over by my partner in the ER.

3—a person whose physical or mental health or strength has suffered damage or has failed. as in: my body, my flailed chest, bruised heart & brain, that bit of lung punctured & collapsed, the lack of sensitivity in my left shin; as in: sometimes I cry, sometimes from pain because I cannot raise myself up from the bed or lift my hands up to my face, sometimes because the opiates harden the shit in my bowels & inhibit peristalsis & my body is too bruised to force contractions, sometimes because I'm tired & my heart feels heavy & my lungs feel heavy & these are not metaphors, sometimes because I now anger easily with my children, sometimes because I'm simply happy to be alive, sometimes because I'm just sad & this sadness is hard to shake.

4—the disorganized remains of something that has suffered damage. as in: this poem. because, though true, I cry for no good reason, all those unknowns & whatifs, all those shards of glass & twisted metal I now carry with me, all that luck & math & grace… & grace… & grace is what I have been given. though I do not how you have fared beyond your ruin of an unregistered, uninsured car that was not yours & those minor bruises you sustained, I was delivered into the hands of a woman & of children that have worried over me & tended to me as if I were a precious gift. & such is life, a gift. & though hackneyed & clichéd, I do not care, I hold that gift more lightly now & more aware. & I wish on you my wretchedness. that in your suffering & exile you would have a family to wrap & bind you in the gentle hug of a seven year-old boy, that you would be taken in by the soft hands of a ten year-old girl as she wipes away your tears, that you would have a partner who will wake in the night & wrap you in a sheet & pull you from the bed so you can pee & feed you watermelon & yogurt when you wake & who will cry in another room because she needs to be strong for you. may we all be so wretched. may the cloaked executioner, the avenging knight wreak love upon each of us. may all your wrack & ruin be the gift of grace.

MY COMPANION 1994 – 2008
by Linda Caldwell

remains in a box
I am afraid to open
babe's ashy bones

RED BUD
by Barbara Sabol

    Since that season of winter thunder
we expect our red bud will become
a collection of kindling—wizened trunk
home to flicker or nuthatch; like us,
inventing new ways to remain useful.

    Yet each April, it exudes
implausible purples, despite
that long-ago lightning blazoned
down its gnarled length, setting the blossoms
more aglow.

    After its bloom, an illusion
of small green hearts, will appear
from nowhere
                           and everywhere.

THIRST
by Jay McCoy

drizzle
douse
drench
drown

seed
saturate
soak
sodden

flash
drop
deluge
steep

splash
spate
slosh
shower

torrent
pour
storm
burst

engulf
immerse
submerge
quench

MAY ALLURE
by Michayla Gatsos

Stand in a field
Look through strands of hair in your face
Trees waver in Flamenco, shimmer in underwater breeze
The forest summons.
Stand in the ocean
Listen through waves
Water whispers loud then decrescendos
The sea pulls.

WET FEET
by T.D. Worthington

Dew
between toes
under heel
wet grass
clinging to skin

Sometimes
wet feet
aint so bad

MADRIGAL
by Sherry Chandler

In the orchard, the Mayapple's "foot-leaf" is turning brown.
The grass where the fawn lay hidden springs up again.
The rictus of laughter is so like the rictus of pain.

The red-lipped frown drawn on the face of a clown
frightens the child, who sees our nakedness plain.
In the orchard, the Mayapple's "foot-leaf" is turning brown.
The grass where the fawn lay hidden springs up again.

We touch him, as we'd touch Jesus or Elvis, to sound
a pitch of his magic as dry earth sounds the rain
singing all the world loves a high stakes game.
In the orchard, the Mayapple's "foot-leaf" is turning brown.
The grass where the fawn lay hidden springs up again.
The rictus of laughter is so like the rictus of pain.

ON THE HILL ABOVE THE RIVER, BIG SYCAMORES BEND
by Unwit

On the hill above the river, big sycamores bend to watch for frogs.
Soft clouds fling ball-bearing-hard water drops. The river's broken face
shimmers like a gong, hand-hammered.

Semis whisper from the highway, make a straight line
away from here in both directions.

Everything happens at once.
None of it makes any sense.

They're out there talking in a language I can't remember.
That's OK.

Somewhere in me knows what's said,
what's whispered and flung in hard handfuls.

Somewhere in me knows what moves without a word, what keeps
    moving
after I can no longer see it, or hear it, or remember its name.

SEQUOIADENDRON GIGANTEUM
by Beatrice Underwood-Sweet

Despite the clearly marked signs,
my father carried a pinecone secreted in his camera bag
from the thicket of trees of Tuolomne Grove
home to rest in Kentucky Bluegrass.

A Sequoia doesn't thrive in Kentucky's
humid summers. It longs for winter dark and deep.
My father will not live to see it
grow tall enough to tower over him.

I imagine a Sequoia would be
lonely without its grove.
Buildings are no companion for trees.
Neither are men, tiny figures
beneath the notice of such a colossus.

I'd rather think of the Sequoias gathered
in Yosemite, whispering and rustling
to one another while I walk around and
through their trunks.

I am fleeting and insignificant
against their lofty and enduring heights.

FOUND PARADOX
by Mary L Allen

Signs
on Alumni Drive
at Tates Creek Road

 "Church Access Only"
"Arboretum Access Only"

BRAD PITT STANDS IN A STORM
by Rain E. Palmer

A soft choir of rain
manifests the skye entire.

If you look real hard
you can see the figure

of a man conducting,
his hands in fists

and for a moment
you'd think he was fighting.

CONTRA.
by Hannah Bishop

Spinning
the room was spinning
even when I was sure I wasn't
Thank god he knew what he was doing
I could barely keep my feet

Dancing
we were dancing
if you could call it that
Over the music, my apologies
this is my first time

Looking
he was looking
right into my eyes
Loss of breath caused by contact
more so than the dancing

BELTED KINGFISHER
by Amy Camuglia

blue mohawk, black tie
high-wire master, fish catcher
helicopter voice

THE COYOTE
by Erin Chandler

How is that aging, cragly head today sir?
How goes that wild grey mane smelling of smoke?
Your pissed off thin lips that spew venom?

The wild ride didn't do a whole lot of good in the end
Congrats though, you became your muse

SHIVA, HER STATUE
by Bernard Deville

Shiva, Her Statue
sits and spears the images
      pouring from the cacophony
        too quickly to get down
        on the two dimensional
        wreckage of paper
      I attempt to crinkle
into some sort of container
for my words.

Tasting
from her trident
those phrases
on the tip
of my tongue.

MY BODY // MY WARZONE: FINGERS
by Allie Marini

five fingers splayed outward // a starfish at the end of my forearm // a weird coral blooming // from phalange bone & tendon, // articulating centrifugal // from shoulder to elbow to wrist, // this abduction of musculature // is how you become a hand // & not a starfish, // not a star, // more than just a five-pointed bit of flesh. // this one points & pulls triggers, // it can also // elicit the gag which breeds beauty, // the thinness // of a watery image // reflected back in porcelain, // on your knees as if in prayer. this one // is not ladylike to raise. // to do so is an act of war. // this one is for marrying, // on your knees again. // pray he likes it & puts a ring on it, // so the whole world // will know your worth. // this one on the end, // learn to crook it politely while drinking— // the pinky finger // tilted ever so slightly // shows that you come from manners, // you were born with class. // this last opposable digit, // terminal extremity, this is the one // that allows you the use of tools. // the one that helps you build things // or break them down to bits again. // four of the stretches of your starfish overcome basic biology // & become something beautiful. // one reminds you that you're part primate, // now & always.

A NEW HAIR CUT
by Heather Dent

Shorn.
That was the word that came to mind
as the hair clippers moved repeatedly
across my vulnerable scalp.

Shorn.
It sounded so harsh,
a word you might use to describe
Nazis shaving the heads
of their Holocaust victims.

Shorn.
Fistfuls of thick red hair
tumbled to the kitchen floor
in graceful spirals,
leaving my head
cold,
bare,
naked.

I looked at the 18 inches of hair on the floor,
then looked in the mirror.

Staring in to my reflection
I did not think,
Shorn.
I did not think,
Victim.
I did not think,
Eww.

I thought,
Strong.

I thought,
independent.
I thought,
hot.

It's nice to know that it was not my hair that made me beautiful.
It was me all along.

THE CLIENT
by c.l. kirby

alien-woman
she watches you
from across the table

she imagines what
it would be like
to overtake your body

to live life through
your senses

to go home
to your bed
to make love
to the man in it

to pull a towel
tight over your breasts
after a warm shower

to comb through
dripping, untangled hair

to catch a glimpse
of yourself in the bathroom mirror
as you lotion your legs

how beautiful!
to smile to yourself and think
yes, I belong in this world

HYPERLEXIA
by M J Eaton

They are following me
 (I see them out of corner of my eye)
I stop
I look
they look back
quickly
then disappear
or stick
this is ridiculous
it is a cereal box
it is a sign that is always there on the wall
an old book (like A TREE GROWS IN BROOKLYN)
I can't go anywhere
without them
they were born with me
they have lived with me
I recognized them first
when I was two
began to put them together
at three
because of print
they don't have to die
with me
but then
I can relax.

MORNING WALK
by Rudy Thomas

Before daylight can chase
night to its death,
I walk alone,

chilled to the bone.
Watching my breath
rise, I quicken my pace.

Never have I seen
birds so tame on the ground.
I come so close to one

I could easily
reach down
& put salt on its tail.

TO LIZ ON THE ROAD
by B.David Perry

On her birthday, today, from Frankfort, she
loaded her 86-year old mother into a Chevy
Cruze and set out for a wedding in Tulsa;
22 years ago, in a Boardwalk Lounge
we met, lives apart…overwhelmed by
barley, we sunk lower yet to that old
shackin' spot, The Robins Nest on
North Broadway, an active train track
close behind the rooms and virtually
zero sleep that night. Tonight, somewhere
west of St. Louis she found a Comfort Inn;
yes, the opossum, his crescent shaped
smile and bare tail gone missing from the site
of last night's slam–Millie nosing through
newly mowed clover, but the
robins, their red breasts beating out
song were tiered in deep canopy along the
out-slope of the abandoned rail-bed.

CRICKET
by Joshua Moore

CHRIST! Will you shut up already?
Really, I'm getting tired of having to
Imagine your body draped in spray,
Cooking like a slice of bacon as you
Know your final day living with your
Exoskeleton has arrived, without a
Tree to which to flee.

OBSCENITIES #2, #3, #4
by Jiv Johnson

OBSCENITY NUMBER TWO

When pigs are executed to be eaten
                                      (at dinner tables)
there's no necessity for a large caliber gun
                                      (certainly not)
buy a .22 caliber at the gun store near the Bath county line
                                      (it's not much of a drive)
bullet into the skull and out the back is enough
                                      (butchers hope so)
so all that is left is the jugular vein on the neck
                                      (one good firm cut)
lay it there to bleed out in the floor for a little while
                                      (it's all a mess)
                Eat tonight at the dinner
                table; between their faces
                the way veins are cut is
                topic of the night. Pass the
                pork, break a wrist.

OBSCENITY NUMBER THREE

The bed sheets are the color of a butcher's apron after a good day of work.

OBSCENITY NUMBER FOUR

I am having nightmares after dinner.
Pounding in the walls
they say it's haunted sometimes
when the farmer and his wife
are home together

to babysit me. That is what
I am here for.
                      a red ghost falls from
                      the farmer's wife
                      when I pass their door.
                      shrieking, the wife eats
                      all of him whole.

HEADLINES AND A DREAM (ZUIHITSU)
by Douglas E. Self

There's a giant hole that's draining a lake on the border of Oklahoma and Texas like it's a bathtub.

I walk in a subway tunnel or a post-apocalyptic underground something. Everything the ground is supposed to be is pink. Pink like the flesh in the back of a throat where that little penis shaped thingy hangs. And all of us straight men say we have never had a penis in our mouth. The bubble gum pink ground consists of abrupt mountains and sudden falls; evidence of an earthquake or bomb, or both. I'm not sure where I am or where I am going, but I see my dad in the distance. He stands on a train platform looking in my direction. It's an older platform from a different era, I think. Caroming my way through the almost unfathomable terrain takes longer than expected, but I reach him. His smile is disconcerting.

Feds: West Side drug dealer had customers lined up around the corner – Chicago.

Dad holds up a clear plastic baggie half full of cocaine. His smile is still disconcerting. I grasp and stare at the dangling baggie as if it were the first volume of what the universe knows. My eyes rise to meet my father's eyes, he is gone. The baggie plops in the palm of my hand.

Woman gets flesh-eating bacteria at Dallas mud run, goes blind in one eye.

She stands smiling in silence. It's been a long time since I have seen her. I don't know who she is, but she's important. Her smile, man, her smile is white like the light that beckons us all, only once. Her presence is that of a symphony on my heavy metal soul.

Photo Emerges Of Channing Tatum as a Teenage Bodybuilder.

We stand in a subway car fuselage. The same as I think people ride in New York City and the very same type I have ridden on the elevated trains in Chicago. The poles used for the non-sitting to hold onto catch my attention. They look gritty and wrong as if waiting to throw slivers of humanity into the hand of each unsuspecting stander that grasps. She is gone. The subway car is moving at full speed.

A Georgetown law professor just perfectly captured the absurdity of Confederate pride.

I don't understand how the subway car is moving when it's not connected to the rails or the rest of the train; even so, the car is in motion. The post-apocalyptic landscape matters not. It seems to have a mind of its own. There are no stops on this route. The car climbs the jagged mountains, and falls. Climbs the jagged mountains, and falls. Climbs the jagged mountains—and falls.

Fertility—Freeze young men's sperm to avoid genetic disorders, says scientist.

I wish I knew where my dad is. I wish she would come back, and I seem to have misplaced the bag of coke.

ELEVATOR CONVERSATION
by Joseph Camuglia

So she says to me,
What? You don't like little dogs?
Little barking dogs.

SHI-I-N: THE SOUND OF NOTHING
by Chuck Clenney

In Japanese
There is a word
That means
The sound of nothing:

しいん (Shi-i-n)
今音を聞こえない (Now, I can't hear a sound.)
しいん (Shi-i-n)
空気が何でもない (The air is nothing.)

At my first Japanese funeral,
I asked a fellow teacher,
"What should I say to
The principal, who lost his mother?"

He said,
"There is a feeling
That silence
Means everything."

It is amazing
That sometimes
Nothing is something,
Something is everything

Nothing is everything
and
                        Everything is nothing.

The Father

THE MATERNITY WARD
by Serena Devi

so much love hurt and bodily fluids

were layered against the stark
backdrop

wings, jars of those different fruits
weigh heavy against one another
glass and ripe matter in some sort
of disorder, if you can even
find them in the blinding white

there's a renoir print on the wall
near the outskirts of the maternity
ward and you wonder
how many babies had their
first synapses form at the rush
of pastel paint and how many
mothers saw snakes beneath the
european woman's petticoat

you don't know whether to look at
the flowers in the foreground or back
you don't know what to see or how
to keep these flowers forever.

I WANT TO BUILD
by Andrew Depew

I want to build a river
something for all of our friends,
the ones who like bathing suits
and making me feel uncomfortable.
The ones who like skiing
and making me feel inadequate.

I'll put it in the street next to the apartment,
so that the neighbors can all enjoy it.
I've organized a ferry for them to get to work.
I got a guy named Clay to run it.

We're themed, baby.

I will build walls to keep the water in.
I'll ask for rain, dance for it, bargain for it
but I will get it.
Our neighborhood will fill up like a tub.

I've set up a drift or ride
so we can receive visitors
by way of
back floating or tubing

I want to build a river.
Something to name after myself.
Something strong, that will cause erosion
leaving my name on the earth.

THE INVISIBLE MAN AT THE GROCER
by Robert S. King

You'd think an invisible man
would have no trouble staying
out of sight, but I always get
the squeaky wheel, cause panic
and frantic security guards.
Nervous shoppers swear
the cart self-propels, that
shaking cereal boxes, heavy cola
cases, and lettuce heads leap
into the buggy. A flying frozen
pizza prompts a UFO report.

My money is invisible too,
so I no longer perform magic
with a cart, never check out, never
incite sirens arresting bags
swaying home on their own.

Instead, I nibble away the day
in a grocery aisle. An energy drink
empties into thin air, a sandwich
bites itself repeatedly, a plastic
fork and spoon defy gravity,
dance in the air face high.
Some shoppers flee, some
gather to watch this miracle,
surely proof of God.

LUCIFEROUS
by Joseph Allen Nichols

Closer.

        look closer.

when the damp & dark of summer night
melts heavy, humid,

        I am flashing,

   flickering,

desperate   yellow-green   light

like Gatsby's distant beacon

     mixing the very breath   I draw

with alchemy, and life blood

        butterflies & luciferin

calling   to you   across   fields

begging   you   to see

    my love   my love

& one little beetle, breaking ground, breaking
my body, burning & incantatory

one of a thousand, yes,
but one of a thousand, hoping

my dance   my song   my flash

     might   convince   you

above   &   falling

    I am a star, too.

AT THE COMPANY PICNIC
by Don Boes

After the volleyball game
the volunteer clown

slips off his incredible shoes.
He's cheerful after awarding

key chains to the kids
while the employees frolic

and the cagey managers
chink and ping in the horseshoe pit.

All will sit down together
at the catered meal—

a pork producer's extravaganza
followed by door prizes—

all save the sweaty comic
who has done the best business,

trading trifles for honest amusement,
spending his clowntime wisely.

ONCE, WHEN I WAS YOUR MOTHER
by Liz Prather

The love lines of your hand
as it slipped into mine,
your sensibility, passed to me like a folded fifty,
brought us both luck.
The wheel watched trees die and moons wax
your assurances were ready
should the stars shock space into a question mark.
A load of timber falling off a semi
A bird strike in the engine of an airplane
A syringe of air plunged into a vein
We met your family at Shoney's afterwards
and decided to honeymoon in Pittsburgh.
Now every day I listen to your chest and wipe your face,
my hands never warm from the Convent lace around us
or the hanging dinner plates and Christmas balls
that I watch, a quarter mile down the road when
I arrive, soon to be with you.

THE GREAT GREY
by Jude Lally

It takes more than a little roadwork,
more than a little detour, to deter me.
I don't know who Greg Page was but
I am familiar with these apartments
I've come upon, which bear his
name, for I lived here when I first
started college 15 years ago so
I know the arboretum is less than
100 yards away. I briefly roll over an
unfinished gravel path, through a patch
of finely manicured grass and onto a paved
walkway, which is what I remember from
my days here as a late-teen. I wander around
the track, past parents and children, baby
strollers and dogs on leashes. I meet
the photographer I'm supposed to meet
with and we make our way under a gingko
tree, listening to the birds and the breeze
and the train in the distance. It's a magnificent
Sunday, a day in memory of the great grey,
Walt Whitman, on his birthday.

INSIDE A FRAGILE BODY
by Pat Owen

And wasn't that he
on the bike yesterday
in the heart of downtown's
rush hour traffic?
I was struck by how thin,
almost frail, he looked
but how you could feel
the charge of his energy
generating out–

a crisp salute to a motorist,
a forceful left hand turn signal–
his whole body vibrating will,
intention.

And he turned
weaving among
the trucks,
construction vans,
honking cars.

THINKING OF ABRAHAM
by Jonel Sallee

Story has it that Abraham saw
A sky full of stars one night—

And what a night that must have been for an old man,
So full as it was of outrageous promise!
Vast progeny, as many as the uncountable stars!
Although, as we know, he had no child
At the time, yet he believed,
We must assume, and —the story doesn't tell us,
Of course—but I imagine his old heart
Must have quickened at so grand a thought!
Can he see now, do you think, across the millennia,
Those stars, that progeny,
Light after light
Birthing, dividing, destroying,
Burning out—
Burning—
I don't know whether such things as time travel are real—
We know so little of our own minds—
Whether, centuries from now, any of us could look back
From one point in our human stories to another,
See some thread, some pattern,
In other words, see
What has come of us.
But if we can,
If Abraham can,
I wonder what that heart of his must feel
Now.

HE WANTS A HANGOVER
by Bronson O'Quinn

so that he can feel bad
without having to hurt
someone

MY MOTHER WRITES ABOUT MY FATHER'S DEATH
by Pauletta Hansel

I see him in his chair
covered with the white
bedspread I made. It seemed
to me he smiled
his little crooked smile
and winked at me.
I caught
a wisp of scent of him
as he floated by
and thought
no matter
that his feet don't work,
he doesn't need them
anymore.

Found poem from writings in my mother's notebook.

A WOMAN'S SHEPHERD
by Elizabeth Beck

> To [my father's] doctrines I owe my great and glorious ambition for the sex to which I proudly belong and whose independence I shall defend until my dying day.
>
> —Rosa Bonheur

I had to learn to celebrate the cow
when first I became a mother and
then, dragged kicking and screaming
to Kentucky where pastoralism no
longer a fleeting afternoon spent
on Shakedown Street at Grateful Dead
shows, but a lifetime of Bluegrass. I
would drive my son home from school
past the farms to look for *our* cows.
My son imagined creating sunglasses
big enough to fit their brown cow eyes
and I would laugh when I first taught
your art to teenagers, calling you and me
both *friend of the cow.* I did not know at
the time that you were also a feminist,
smoking cigarettes and cutting your hair
short. And it is not without irony that I,
too, believe all animals to have a soul.
Even as I cut into my steak.

PAINTED NAILS PROVE
by Lucia Cherciu

that woman is meant for decoration
to hold her hands out suavely
and not touch anything
so the nail polish doesn't smudge
or chip away.

That she's not supposed to get
deep into the matter of things,
like knead focaccia dough with rosemary
slosh potatoes with olive oil and basil,
or mix freshly chopped savory into meat balls.

That she's supposed to reach out her hands
in front of her as if she's showing off her ring
as if her hands were her mirror and not her deeds;
what she looks like, not what she does;
what she can buy, not what she thinks.

That she's not supposed to dig in the dirt
to plant new sage and thyme,
chamomile and mint,
or weed gladiolas and dahlias,
transplant cosmos and zinnias.

That she's not supposed
to hold her newborn on her bare chest
because her long nails might scratch
his skin newly out of the waters
of Creation.

THE BRAIN IS NOT THE MIND
by Alx Johns

Anyone with an aquarium can see
that any study on the duration
of fish memory

is bullshit.

Ten seconds, my ass.

They rush to the glass whenever they see my face;
they recognize their god and know
the source of their food,

and they love when my eyes
form from silently present,
unaccessed hope

to grey blur to
ghostly shape to
clearly the one we
remember,

who sent the manna last time

snowing down in elegant slow motion
just enough to satiate
but never pollute the tank.

Thanks displayed solely in the golden dance
of dining with the joy of multiplied loaves.
When they pass before the light,

I can see right through
to the soft dark shadow
of their hearts.

CALL IT DESTINY
by Katrin Flores

Sometimes,
one finds her calling
when she can down a
quesadilla
while watching
a forensic anthropologist
sift through a concoction of
gelatinized bone and flesh
with a soup ladle,
and bile does not
coat her throat.

IT ALL ADDS UP
by Tina Parker

I kill a black widow outside my front door
My lunch order rings up to $6.66
I steal a pen and legal pad from work
And take them into the restaurant
Where I eat dinner alone on my 40th birthday
It's my favorite restaurant and I sit
By a floor to ceiling window
I watch hipsters hurry to and from yoga
I watch a dad rest his hand on his toddler's head
I watch a bird build a nest in a stripped-out meter box
The days-long cloud cover lifts and the evening sun shines
Into the window at such an angle it feels like a gift.

YOU = TIME MACHINE
by Lennart Lundh

It's as though you were a time traveler,
showing up in my life unexpectedly
and then leaving, again and again.

The cat in the photograph is dead now,
as are the flowers in the vase,
the bird in the tree outside the window.

It's not that I want them to be absent,
or that they did. They had no say in the matter,
no more than I might, stranded here forever.

The picture is as old as my memories of times,
so they and I have no hope for resurrection.
Unless, of course, you bring them back with you.

DAD TELLS US WE ARE RAISING ONLY FIVE ACRES THIS YEAR, AN ACRE HERE, AN ACRE THERE

by Melva Sue Priddy

By the time I am eight
I know an acre in a bottom
just by looking.
I know a hillside acre.
I know an acre ridding
alongside-the-road.
I know an acre split by a pond.
I know a neighbor's acre.
I know an acre hung in the pole barn.
I know an acre of alfalfa.
An acre of baled hay stored,
that varies more than anything else.
Dad calls it an acre
but I know, from my years
of looking, this
sure as hot rocks
is more than any acre
of plowed ground. More
like two and a half.

WHAT MY FATHER FELT
by ashley parker owens

I guess what my father felt
blue flashing lights
hearing a yell, running steps
pulling a hard curtain aside to look out the window
stepping out the door into humid cool air
early summer morning
emergency personnel at the pool
a small crowd
backdrop of people staring out windows
I get it, a child drowned
the same age as me

what is harder to understand
is how I felt
not allowed to go on a
school trip on a boat
because if it capsized
parents would save their own
and not me

alone in a classroom
teacher's aide cleaning
windex sprayed on
desks and white board and chairs
ceiling lights powered off
but ample dull light
confined to a desk
nothing to do
but think about what I felt
alone and sad and punished
for what my father felt

SCARLET RIBBONS
by K. Bruce Florence

Dad, never bent to women's work
Had no heart for frills and fuss.
Wide shoulders, hard hands,
Coal miner's strength and
Iron willed enough to find his
His way to work on top
While others rode the mantrip.

I never dared to think he paid
Me any of his man mind.
Then a plague of fever hit the kids
On every ridge and down the road.
Too fast for wake, funeral, tears.
Choking grief shocked, silenced us.

When the fever raced through me.
Mother shrieked and began to grieve
And left Daddy all night to watch me die.
Kerosene heat, threw ghosts across
The ceiling and cocooned us.
While he fought the demon
I drowsed–fever drunk, hot.
He pitted his grit against my life
Ebbing into scarlet ribbons.

The doctor barked, "Make it to morning.
There's nothing left to do."
And once again, "Make it to day."
Daddy clenched his jaw,
 "We'll make it, Doc."
He took my hand in cool, easy fingers

And whispered, "She's my girl.
No one gets her, not even the angels."

WHY I AM RETICENT
by J. Wise

I know hard eyes like those, stoney and burning.
When they go out, they don't leave
a void, like other fires. They leave something akin
to black holes, dark and gaping maws
of fathomless cruelty,
slowly tearing apart
anything stupid enough
to cross into their event horizon.

ALL THE NIGHT STARS
by Linda Caldwell

Dorritt Hufflet, who decades ago
tabulated every visible star from earth,
numbered them 10,000.

For me, counting stars becomes easier each year.
With my naked eye frozen to the gray night above,
I am fortunate to see the summer triangle in July
and Orion in October.

DAY 25
by Lynnell Edwards

Whose gemstone is rain.

Or the threat of rain, something else
I still don't know the answer to

on the horizon and blowing
across the sky. Its stony cape

bulges, and at the hem weak
light like yesterday's news,

the already solved world, what we
thought we saw coming.

IN MOTION
by Jeffrey Helton

When I read you Rumi,
he speaks back,
a hysterical silence
that roves your spine
and shimmers the leaves,
lemon-yellow with light,
your laughter carrying
the powder of his bones.

When I meditate, aware only
of your breath, the same
seaswell breath of treetops,
how Sufjan sings.
These arpeggios like feathers
for the birdsong.

When the ant scales a
tall blade of grass,
his body like grapes by firelight,
he marvels at your bare legs,
like white dunes of
a world in motion.

ASK AND YE SHALL
by Luke Wallin

there's a leap second coming tonight

clocks listen up, skip a beat
moon drag is pumping the sea
slowing the planet and writers like me

if clocks don't obey what i say
in 800 years, well guess what
instead of high noon when it's done
gary cooper will draw at high one

last second to midnight you'll jump
pretending you made a mistake
assuming earth's party rocked on
while you sleeping clockie were gone

ho ho pocketwatches, sundials
a swish for the pendulum's swing
did i hear you say radioactive decay
we'll put our plus second in play

some will lend it to Greek hesitation
some will use it to prolong a kiss
go for the score, don't try to store
didn't you beg for just one second more

midnight will bring syncopation
Lexpo's season will gracefully close
codas are fine, now to tonic with lime
writers be pleased with our wee extra time

CHILDREN OF ABRAHAM DEBATE GLORIFICATION
by Bobby Steve Baker

what life do you have
for this one you call I Am

                                  that that is—
                                  is

do you take what is mine
do you give it away

                                  that that is not
                                  is not

you are a woman
do you have free will

                                  is it not so

no—your father chose your fate—
are you a fool

                                  it is so

I will hold you I am entitled to you
you will bear children a son

                                  that that is not
                                  is not

one worthy of my name
this is the will of the Prophet

                                  is it

do you think the grip of my power
is weakening

                                  it is

do you claim freedom without me
as you are—as I am

                                  that that is
                                  is

without me you will be nothing

                                  that that is not
                                  is not

MURDER MY MACHISMO
by Alex Simand

The way you say brown shower, like it's
a cute Mexican restaurant that just opened
& not the act of shitting on someone
(for money), I guess that triggered me.
It's one thing to have casual sex, an entirely
different beast to be casual *about* sex,
to laugh about clothespin zippers,
canes, whips, nipple clamps, crops,
hooks, rings, Prince Alberts, leather masks
& all manner of dungeon tool in your drawer
I lack a vocabulary to describe. You're my
fifth grade English teacher who gifted me
a tattered copy of Don Quixote.

I used to think it perversion: I owned
an aversion to sex in the shadows,
the kind of acts performed on, not with.
I never considered the glee of catharsis,
that tears might at once harm and please,
that red inflammation is worn with pride,
marks like trophies you point to and say
This is where I hurt; this is where I feel.
Like maybe control is a concept best left
to DMV queues & boardroom meetings.
When we fuck we are animals, blood
spilling on bathroom floors. Your skin,
your soul is made to stretch.
I am the vanilla in Neapolitan, but my white
abuts browns, pinks, melts together
if you leave me out long enough.
My manliness blurs when you push my knees

far enough behind my ears: a capsized turtle
resigned & delirious to my unseen fate.
Things look a little different from here.
Up seems like down, stoicism like weakness,
fingers like nails, the insistent screeching
of a chalkboard becomes a loving embrace.
So do it—embrace me, show me impossible
angles, let me cry in fevered agony.
When we're done I'll still have my feet
unless you take them, too.

The Son

GO
by Jennifer Barricklow

five days have I come
down to water's edge
and bowed, head touching
knees, so that the fifth
day I might begin

the long journey home

* *go* is the word for the numeral five in Japanese

GABE: A REQUEST OF YOUR PRESENCE
by Rae Cobbs

This Fourth, my son, beloved, leave the bottle
capped, let the can, unpopped, stay sealed.
They'll always be around to tempt you: just for
a holiday, force your mind open, your eyes to see.
Let the guarded gestures soften, love emerge.

My dog's asleep, wagging her tail, rolling her eyes,
remembering some happy chase in dreams.
Your family will remember going through
the motions of backyard barbeque, potato salad,
bright cut vegetables, a bought cherry pie.

You can gather toward yourself the remnants
of splintered years. They want your steady hand
lighting the punk, gently telling them to stand back.
Maybe they'll embrace the prodigal father, mate,
and friend. Maybe it will still be stiff, chin away.

It's true, I'll always love you, but night after night
I dream I'm losing you. My mate wakes me because
I holler. I watch you climb away and fall: no matter
how I strain, you slip away. I feel the greatest loss
I've known, and it is multiplied by siblings, cousins,

Grampa, uncles, aunts, your chosen family, friends.
What we don't ask is that you turn around, fight
to come back because you love us, too. I'm asking,
now: forgive us all our absences, distractions, and
mistakes. We wanted you to find yourself, unfettered:

Now we want you back, yourself. Maybe it will feel
so good, you'll stay, already forgiven, son. If we get
it wrong, we'll laugh. Maybe we all will cry. It could

get the lava moving, let off steam. There are years
ahead for you to be the self you are, my cherished one.

DEAD ARTIST'S DAUGHTER
by Erin Mathews

I'm sorry

Because it's not fair
to be signed up
as living exhibit
against your will

DAUGHTER
by Christopher McCurry

If tucked
like black opal
somewhere
in the body's
carmine
is a soul,
leave it be.

It's a useless
thing. No trinket
for a chain.

You can do
so much more
with your hands
than worry
a small stone.

OVERLY CONCERNED

by hb elam

all my life, every

one
every group
every body
has been
    overly concerned
with my body
and what I do with it

why do you care
who I am
who I love
who I fuck
fuck you, every
body
who tries to control my
body

"is that a boy
or a girl, I can't tell"
as if I must be either/or

"I heard he likes
*insert male
genitalia
euphemism here*"
as if I must be
delimited
by what I put in my mouth

my god judges me
not by what I put in

my mouth but by
what comes out

I wouldn't come out,
crying under the covers, my mother
telling me maybe it's "just a phase"
asking me if I had "experimented"
and the shakes of my head
under covers
in the darkness
shook her to the core

split her son
into two
one half hers
and the other not
some foreigner inhabiting
what once inhabited her

we do not talk of such things
we do not talk much at all
they do not ask about my "sex life"
we never had "the talk"

forced to rely on the network
of information too tempting to resist
of chat rooms where I bared a soul
my parents refuse to see

I am an "abomination"
I have "intimacy issues"
I "hook up"
I "sin"

when he puts it in
and the real me comes out
too scared to be him
around them
around anyone

I don't feel much of anything
anymore, as if I ever did
playing a part in a play
that you wouldn't let me write

I didn't audition
for this
for any of it
this life, your life
and you won't let me out
either

I'm out, I'm done
I'm me and I won't fall in
 line
in your line anymore

fuck you

I was never overly concerned with you
or
your opinion
anyway

LITTLE A
by Joan Burke

oh my baby, little
girl with my lipstick on
what
I'd give to go back
crouch down, hold you
little kisses from tiny lips
so sweet, soft little arms, tangled hair
everywhere you are so small!
one more hug
you smell like that baby I couldn't
believe was mine
clutching two of my fingers
you lurch into your wild joy-run
your shoe flew off
you let it go so
I could go back
get it
for you.

SOFT
by Stevie Farmer

I can be both girl and disaster
Daisies growing from the open wounds on my knees
                Like roots pushing through concrete
Nothing about me is unyielding
Try and tell me that it does not make me stronger
                Letting life weave its way through me
I am not breaking apart
I am fortified by the love I let in
Filling the cracks in my bones with
                        Flowers

I STARE
by Christopher Miller

at my hands,
consider meandering
veins and fissures
etched into palms by time.

These cannot be my hands.

The hands
that flew the Millennium Falcon
in a daring attack on my
sister's Barbie Dream
House, made

a diving catch
in the fourth inning,
struck out in the ninth,
chased away victory,

won a two-punch bout,
a black eye my best friend
blamed on a basketball
to save the rest of his face.

The hands
that wrestled steel strings
pulled taut over rosewood,
strained to coax a reluctant
'Am I Evil' out of cheap frets,

wrote a speech to mark
the advent of tomorrow.
Student and parent wept
while the principal checked
his watch, celebrated the end

of a lifetime of temperance
by raising the first beer
to accomplice lips,

belied false bravado as
they quivered at the
timid first touch of
a woman's breast.

The hands
that, in moments
of unflinching betrayal,
wielded blades and pills
against their host,

wore a ring with a vow
of forever only to
remove that promise
some years later, stroked

a cat's cheek while
wicking away tears
in the vet's office
as life made its
final exit.

The hands
that now behold
beauty, embrace love
and the universe held
in their midst.

I stare.
These cannot be
my hands.

THE CHANGELING REFLECTS ON A TYLENOL AD
by Elizabeth Burton

On a TV in the Lexington airport
An ad for Tylenol asks me:
"When were you first told
You were faulty?" My first
Thought is: "My, that's a rather
Big question for an over-the-counter
Painkiller to ask," but my second
Is: "It was not so much a telling
As a knowing." I was told
In tight smiles and forced pride
From the people who scooped
Me up for years thinking I was soft
River clay only to realize
That I was limestone. I was told
In the way my friend says,
In a dark car on a darker road,
"I worry about you," and told
Even louder when all I can do is laugh.
I shouldn't invite worry; I can barely
Invite friends over for dinner.
In the old hill-words of my father,
"I've got a screw loose," a fresh-
From-the-factory defect, only
Someone threw away the receipt,
Dazzled by the yellow curls
And blue eyes that would disappear
With my sanguine nature
And good eyesight. Looking
At pictures of me as a baby,
You would never think "Something
Is wrong with her," but, then again,

Me and that little girl
Have very little in common.

BAIT SHOP
by Duke Gatsos

Refuse coagulates inside the belly of earthworms.
A sand flea scurries across the concrete floor,
escapes the stink of hour-dead shrimp.
Feathery flies hang in cellophane,
await application to invisible string.
Tint of metal shines for hook,
weighted to dangle over seaweed.
A boy and his dad jingle the door hanger,
the kid laughs from that unmolested place,
the belly of innocence unaware
of fish carcasses in the freezer.

BROTHER
by Jennifer Beckett

There's you leaning against the Chrysler
on a warm September night, handing me
my first Sufjan Stevens cd, saying
"I know you'll like this."

There we are at the kitchen table
playing Jenga and playing it again
so we could call it "Return of the Jengi."

I can hear those months
when you overused a British accent,
picture that bright green shirt
only you could make look good.

You had the most real smile.

We had so few moments together.
I magnify those memories
until they block out the questions.

Where memory fails,
time beatifies.
I can't stop praying.

THE GRADUATE
by Brittany Castle

You are eighteen,
But you are twenty seven minutes of photos
In a montage set to sentimental country songs.
Mom cries to Billy Dean at the graduation party.
You will turn a once broken home into empty nest
And call it freedom.
I want to steal you away and wrap you up,
Like I did years ago to your action figures.
Casts handmade from Kleenex and tape,
I told you their limbs were broken.

For you, I readied them for battle.

WHERE THE WALL MEETS THE FLOOR
by Sean L Corbin

I use the pry bar to pull
the toe bar from the wall's seam,
revealing the exact point
where these two cracked planes meet
at a ninety-degree angle,
our perpendicularity, once hidden
behind this thin strip of wood,
now exposed to the open air.

LONG OFF WET BELL
by Colin Boyd

Snow colored like Superman
and reggae like Tweety Bird,
the roller rink smells like
the Mystery Machine and
the pier sways like the 70's.
Bright orange and white lights
cover skin and concrete
like face paint and graffiti
with cigarette butts
and pours smothered with sunscreen.
Mint leaves in hair
are blown a long way off
with a pelican formation,
fishing with a rogue wet bell
years below the surface.

ALL NIGHT LONG
by Sue Neufarth Howard

Black crows of the spirit
hover over seemingly
inexhaustible nocturnal
casino zombies
maintaining their
soldierly posture
beneath the blazing
4 a.m. intensity of
electric sun
their jubilant infatuation
with the sonorous
rumble of slots and
gaming wheels
morphed to a
vague fog of
pleasure past tense
slowly slumping toward
unplugged time out
retreating to the temporary
bourgeois comforts of
zonked out rest
before the glitz
of the green dream
pursuit renewed

TOO HAPPY SO I,
by J. L. Taylor

it started out like
this

a hard letter
in between teeth-
i ask you,
do your jaws pop
with tight pink
bubble-gum?

grazing your eyes
at me funny
thin freckles crease
into light dimples
and look at me funny

no
you say
no they don't
pop

I said
my jaw dances the wrong
way
as unorthodox as
pubescent teens at cotillion

she said
maybe go see a doctor

i agreed with
my head tilted towards her
let her walk where

she'd soon forget me
but still could see
my queer figure

across the way
i stammered
thank you!
in her thumbed shadow

thank you
for suggesting
that my jawline might
be in trouble
but at least i finally
have something
to worry about

HAT TRICK DIADEM
by meadowdawn

a chosen minority,
weighed and measured.
spirited riders, of bridled beasts.
teaming with flair,
profoundly poised,
all risks assumed for the pleasure of kings.

male jockeys are to petite four, what other men are to cake.

HARD YEAR
by Maggie Brewer

Tyrell:
When he analyzed "The Kiss" by Klimt
he wrote,"my momma should be
    treated better."
He told us, "I'm from
    Ferguson,
this is nothing."
When the verdict came
      he was quiet.

Kendrick:
He and his girl are having
    trouble.
She won't tell her parents
about him.
The football player
dad would love,
yes, m'am gentleman
mom would trust,
who they will never know.

Austin:
Says "they" and "them" in
    Baltimore
Are "so stupid to riot."
Hat, shirt, cell phone
bear the
      Confederate Flag.

Delaysia:
Her daddy is a preacher.

She was raised
    in Philadelphia.
Lost friends and
     family this year
but laughs when
    she's uncomfortable.

Me:
I don't watch the news,
still I see the videos,
    they just keep coming,
from city after city.
My wife is crying,
    worried about our friends,
and through her tears
she whispers,
       "I can't breathe."

FILLER
by Randall Walden

I am no one entirely to myself.
But I will try to sleep this one off.
Just don't try to put your
faith into shooting stars.

Anyways, it's probably asteroid shit.

PATCHWORK WOMAN
by Bianca Lynne Spriggs

> after "Grande Odalisque" by Jean Auguste Dominique Ingres (1814)
>
> One critic remarked that the work had "neither bones nor muscle, neither blood, nor life, nor relief, indeed nothing that constitutes imitation"
>
> —Roger Benjamin, "Ingres Chez Les Fauves" (2000)

She wasn't from around here.
He found skin for her
in the butterfly bush
beneath his studio window,
spread out over the dazzling
wingcloth of three dozen
small whites lolling around
the nectar beneath a June sun.
He took them all home, crushed
them and made a reflective paste
of their wings, smeared it
along her cheekbones.
Her back. Her ankles.
Her limbs were thin
branches out in the yard
blown down by last night's storm.
Elm. Sycamore. Holly.
Her fingers and ankles, cutlery,
a couple pieces of flatware.
He wired together what he could
and poured taper wax
over where muscle met bone.
Her hair—he stole
from the mare, snipped
the length of her umber tail
as she stood asleep,

dreaming of fallen apples.
He borrowed the fan
from a neighbor,
but she didn't know it.
The scarf came from
another neighbor's
brocade couch, tassel and all.
The visible eye,
was one of his own,
plucked out and left
to temporarily wander around
in her skull—he didn't even
wince when he did it.
Just painted with one lid shut.
And when they said what they said,
he patted her on her winged
backside and laughed to himself—
what they didn't know
is that she was never alive,
and so what they didn't know
wouldn't kill him.

WORLD CUP STRATEGY FOR THE UNITED STATES
by Gaby Bedetti

To win your first World Cup in 16 years, take risks.
The rest of the world has come to play, too.

No more drumming your fingers during the anthem
or waving to the fans or kissing the goalpost.

Forget the last failed shot. Press high up the field
and dribble at defenders. Show swagger with each possession.

Make probing runs from varied angles. Be fast
and relentless and create surprises.

Have the face of an angel and tackle like a beast.

THE GOOD OF THE GRAPE
by Karlee Caswell

The vineyard is continually filled with grapes,
but there is always one that becomes a raisin
too early.
Or maybe it was always a raisin,
I just never noticed.
When I pick in the vineyard,
I look for grapes,
round,
juicy,
succulent,
grapes.
Boss tells me,
raisins have no flavor,
they got all the good
sucked out.
Grapes are the ones we want
behind the two sets of six white bars
inside us,
he says.
I see many raisins in the world,
you know?
I nod.
You got a big grape
he says,
pointing.
Keep it.
Grapes made wine,
and wine fueled the people.

BEFORE THIS
by Jason Lee Miller

Before this we floated
Our amniotic kingdoms
Sole heirs sucking down the world
Pulling earth and water inward
The primordial clays of Being as
Tiny bits of time through blood

Before this we were schizo
The split-Minds of the cosmic egg
The hanging heuvos, the illusion
Of separation our grandest charade
Because without seeing we both felt
The way grandmother tossed her faithless husband
From a foot log—we were jostled, full of feelings,
The fall
The creek-splash, the sting of shame and fear
We felt, too, how he lay himself down
Before the dozer because to him
Even a country road was a foil for paradise

Before this we ate what they ate
And what they ate carried a little of their blood
But also the nutrients of soil—the shit of worms
That before this was a tick that had sucked down
An entire deer before time wore it smooth enough
That it was ripe for pushing up maters
We drank what they drank—waters pushed up from beneath
That before had scrubbed the salt and metal from time-smoothed rock
And after this traveled down the mountain carrying little bits of everything
Out to sea

Before this we traveled that stream of everything
And we became vapor in the wind
Somewhere over Venezuela maybe, we fell into joyousness
Knowing the comfort of eternal repetition

Before this we traveled the globe this way
Leaving little bits of ourselves all over and seeding it
I was conceived in New Orleans – and also Turkey and Taiwan

Before this our illusion of separation was more perfect
We swirled around as elements spewed from the star

Before this, before we had ears to hear of time or distance
We were hurled, for lack of a better term, out into possibility

Before this we were a word
Before this, a thought
From a Oneness existing even before
An equation developed that might allow it to exist

And before this … well
It might be more useful to talk about after
Back across whatever number it is we can't even write
Back to now and after this
Where we do it again—break apart into worm shit
And spread ourselves around that way
Until yet again we are gathered up
All the tiny separate pieces of us
Some perfect place and time downstream

15.6.30
by GA Smith

Weeks later,
I become an archaeologist
Digging through memos
Written on my phone—

Kisses are temporary
Lip canoodles

—struggling to decipher
Context in half-thoughts
And conversations with
Evan Williams

ALIX DREAMS OF AN END, BUT NOT THE END
by Victoria Sullivan

Under the ballroom door, I watch the flames dancing. I hear their feet crackle against the floor. I hear their heels sizzle. I touch my hair and sob because I cannot join them. Nobody hears except for Nicky, whose eyes have fallen out. The children have started screaming. They wail like the summer storms that railed against the windowpanes in Hesse. I cannot rise from my chair to help them but it does not matter, they are laughing now. Nicky laughs. His forehead bleeds and I wipe it away with my fingers. His blood is black and when I put it to my tongue, it tastes like smoke and sweat. The door groans open and I see the children dancing on the walls, holding hands with the fire. They are still laughing and I bid them go to bed, but their eyes are pearls and their teeth are rubies. Gold pours from their lips and bubbles in their throat, and the flames lift them up onto the chandelier. They bid me come. The fire licks my ankles like a little dog.

a/n: Throughout her life, the Empress Alexandra Romanova (wife to Nicholas II) recorded her dreams as part of her diary–this prose poem borrows from them in style as well as content, as most of her dreams were concerned with her family and their concerns for their safety.

ON A HEARING IN CHARLESTON
by Dorothy Bouzouma

I am wondering why they have brought him here
the skinny angle of his jaw
the mushroom cap of hair
the doleful eyes, bordering on sadness
from the TV screen his skin is not
white
but a pallor of grey
as if this might not be black and white
but instead
the curve of a metaphor
so many shades of grey

It seems unfair
to have to see this face
for a moment I am afraid
of my own sympathy
which rises, acidic and distasteful, in my throat
this skinny little kid
who I can easily see belongs nowhere at all
looking incapable
Incapable
of this horror
he might cry now
for a moment pursing his lips
into lines that squeeze tight
tremble a little

I have rolled over
from a fitful, dreamless sleep
where the sounds of a CNN reel
rolled tumultuously through my fog-filled brain

I have rolled over, rubbing sleep from my eyes
and he stares me down

As I watch
when I am not bordering on sympathy
a strange hysteria bubbles to the surface
and I am afraid I might laugh
aloud, quiet inappropriately
at this moment
where he looks so small and cowardly
knowing he will forever be lonely
seeing him in the tiny square of that room
hands locked behind his back

I wish though instead of him
I might see the victims
their images are displayed alongside his frame
9 little squares
Some of them could be my people
The rounded brown face of my Aunt B
whose voice swelled, without practice,
to fill our little A.ME. church on
Sunday mornings
But the pictures lack imagination
as if they are not real at all
Paper Mache people posted up alongside their killer
They seem to scream for their own space

I wish I could at least see the faces
of the victims' families
who approach one by one
out of the shot of the camera

I cannot see them
So I close my eyes
Stop looking
Start listening
to feel out this story
the shuffle of papers
the steady movement of heavy breath
eyes closed, I can put my finger on this grief
which rises, hot and full, like steam
there is a moan
like a wounded animal
like something giving away
a sob
almost escapes but is pulled back
quick
before we are consumed
the tremor of voices
shake on words
and forgiveness

I might come undone
I am always searching for a reason
I might read Gandhi
who is always full of hope where there is none
but I do not read Gandhi or anyone at all
I smoke a cigarette
and write these words
on the front porch
where rain hits the ground like tears
unfolding like grief

an alternating soft and hard pattern
my eyes are moist and my nose drips uncontrollably

This is a map
This atlas of violence and terror
This chartered course
Leading always back
From where we came
But we are poor navigators
Even poorer readers of history
We cross the same path again and again
An act of cultural insanity

& The Holy Ghost

"OF COURSE THERE'S AN AFTERLIFE"
by Sarah Freligh

—first line from "Tomorrow and Tomorrow" by Kurt Brown

If not, we're on this earth practicing
for nothing, like the pianist locked
away in a dark room playing
scales until his fingers cramp and still
isn't accomplished enough for a solo
show at Carnegie Hall. Yet his music
is beautiful. Notes lilt up, out
of a small window, grace the air
on the avenue below where a woman
is walking her dog who stops, head
cocked, to let the chords christen
his ears. If the pianist dies in his sleep
tonight, what good is practice if there's
no afterlife, no dark corridor to travel
through on the way to a lighted stage?
The audience he dreamed of
is waiting and though their faces
are indistinct, he knows that those
he has loved are there. When
the orchestra soars, maybe that
shiver you feel is the Angel
of Death, fringed wings brushing
your shoulder. Maybe she's
cruising you.

IN THE DIP BEYOND THE UPLAND
by Poetessa Leixyl Kaye Emmerson

At the base of the chalk formation he entered the garden.
He was going to, perhaps, kiss her. Her untidy misgivings
vanished into the ridgeway with greater zest than all the
philosophies, or what not. The vast northern landscape
lay beneath the tenderness, further off than it had seemed.

   —Found Poetry based on the book, "Jude The Obscure"
    by Thomas Hardy, pages 48-49.

CONSTELLATION
by Jonathon La Mar

amazing how light can revise
what the eye will see. a vision:

my lover comes to me disguised
in the form of a man. his wings still
beat wildly behind him, forgotten.

the feathers slice through the air
quiet as a knife. penultimate symbol
of his divinity, the last of the true
body that will not be left behind.

he is the old sort of god—half-
beast and nearly human. he lusts
for his creation as his creation

lusts for him. when his hands touch
my skin, I can see how this will end:

my earthly self come undone
as I burst into a body of stars.

FIVE DIRECTIONS TO MY HOUSE
by Karen George

~ After Juan Felipe Herrera's poem of the same name

1. Cross the river from Ohio to Kentucky. Use the Roebling Suspension Bridge. Notice the twin towers, rope cables, engraved date. 1867.

2. Reflect on borders. Ones you've crossed, ones remaining.

3. If mid-May, inhale the balm of locust blossoms. Pinch a honeysuckle trumpet, slide out the string until the pooled nectar appears. Lick it.

4. Round the lake where scruffy ducklings trail their mother.

5. Press a pulpy leaf of the live-forevers that lean against the limestone slab set on its thin edge–the silhouette of a halibut.

6. Bow to the grey wolf that guards my front door. Praise the wild ones.

OUR TIME
by Vijay Singh

Age of this universe
Is neither five thousand nor
Thirteen point six billion years;
But just this instant
Of light on dewdrop,
Sun rising over horizon

Trillions of years are rolled
Into this moment now present

How sweet then
That you loved me
For so many dewdrops

BELIEVING
by Amanda Kelley

I interviewed a Nazarene preacher once
who said God spoke to him
through scripture
when he happened upon the right passages
at the right time—
I thought it sounded like
throwing a dart at a map
with your eyes closed.

I walked through a used bookstore once
and sat on a stool in the parenting section
looking for something more
than the complete idiot's guide
to blended families—
but then God spoke to me
in the fiction section
when she said,
Now Is the Time to Open Your Heart.

I SLEEP LIKE THE #4
by Debbie Adams Cooper

              in bed on my side like
                     #4
             you used to lie like #8
               hands above head
                         bowed fingers touching
       feet bottoms flat touching, legs
              rounded in a bowl

              together we made
                  12 back
                     then

             we multiplied twice

   now you sleep on the couch like #1
   and in the middle of the night I find
                    you there as #7
   arms outstretched before
                 you

   i'm still #4 in bed at night but
           now I lie with
              #0

WE SLEEP ON PAPER
by Michelle Knickerbocker

The crisp lined sheets
clean and empty
wait to embrace
the soft, tired form;
ready to re-ignite
dreams and quell hunger
after fire-drill orbits
and polished scullery days.
We are gingery thoughts
and lemony emotion,
the ebony inkpot
of smoky imagery laid
onto a bare plate:
Our bed is the poem.

POET IN THE CORNER
by Holly Wooten

"Let's go listen to a poetry reading,"
I said.
You mustered a grin and complied,
but the slight eye roll
couldn't be missed.
Sprawled on a grassy hill
we listened as each verse
sought to compel
a reaction:
shock,
sadness,
sympathy,
longing,
confusion.

We felt nothing.

You joked,
"I have been hurt,
I *have* been hurt!"

It wasn't until the last
poet
stood from the far corner
of the green,
clothes soiled and tattered,
hair and beard ratty.
His hands shook as he read
from his unfolded piece of
lined paper,
eloquently recounting a lost love

dancing barefoot
on a beaten wood floor.

As we listened,
the mouth couldn't help but
to suddenly draw air:
Poetry.

FIRE
by Alexis

It all begins with a spark
that grabs onto the wood
holds on tight
and spreads its warmth throughout the log,
growing higher and higher
while fading into a softer and softer light.

It dances for the log:
performs.
But the audience is getting smaller and smaller.
Their ashes piling up higher and higher.
Until the log is no more
and the flame takes a bow
before slowly fading into
nothingness.

LIFE IN A TEA CUP
by Tara Cremeans-Mounger

The cracks are subtle.
The stains are dark.
Sticky edges where
our lips have met.
Sometimes sweet,
sometimes bitter.
I am consumed.

SESTINA & I
by Aidan Ziliak

I
eat
Bob.
He
smiles,
ravenous.

Ravenously
I
smile.
Eat
him,
Bob.

Bob,
ravenous,
he &
I
eat,
smiling.

Smile,
Bob,
eat.
Ravenous,
I &
he

He
smiles –
I,

Bob,
ravenously
eat.

Eat
him
ravenously,
Smiling.
Bob &
I

Smiling,
eating Bob.
He & I,
ravenous.

HOW WE LIVE LOVE
by Harriet Windsor

> In this
> Precarious unknowing
> We live love.
>
> —Rumi

I live two in one; I live more than that.
You speak of flame, of a burning head to toe;
I, recovering from psych meds, don't feel it.
Not like that. But I reach tendrils toward the flame.
My fingers are strong: they make words and sex.
If I could pleasure you with a gel pen
I would do so with great confidence, all day.

I am seeds of a weed, blown over fields of poppies,
though I experience myself, more, as a stick in a river
of mud. I long for currents, to dislodge me,
to fill my lungs, to fill my eyes with blindness
to the past, to yesterday, even, when you
told me we had never spoken. That big, fat lie
sent me back many lifetimes, to gather my resources.

But listen hard: I am a powerful professional.
I care for Gaia, twenty-four hours a day,
though all I receive as pay is a social security check.
You have shoveled dirt on my remains
and crowed about it. I have been the crazy one.
But when you plant me in the ash pit, I fashion
of myself the spitting image of your Tyger face.

I WILL HEM THE SKIRT OF YOUR PAIN
by Savannah Sipple

stitch it tight, make it light, easier
to haul. Let my hands do this
for you—let them unburden you, peel
that snaked skin new. I will wrap you,
snug from the thing that quickens your pulse,
hold you warm like sun-rubbed sheets.
Let me trim that ache, sew it with *love*
and *safe*. I'll fold you close, one yard at a time.
I'll tuck myself in the raw cotton of you.

THIS MORNING, I LAUGH
by Elizabeth Sands Wise

A wake-up kiss in the morning sounds romantic
unless the recipient startles in his sleep and jerks
away, afraid in the semi-darkness of early alarms,
baby monitors, and white noise machines, afraid
of the sudden presence he senses in front of his face
about to touch his lips.

Years ago, on New Year's morning,
in sleeping bags on a friend's boyfriend's uncomfortable floor,
as I began to wake, I sensed a presence
near my left ear and felt a gentle, tickling breath in my hair.
Turning abruptly to face the apparition, half-doubting
half-believing my own racing heart, I frightened
the cat who froze, briefly, eye to eye with me,
his whiskers on my cheek.
He darted under the piano.

This morning, I laugh
as you lurch away from me in the darkness.
"Happy anniversary," I whisper, still smiling.

I SAW THE FRANK IN HANK AND THEN I SET HIM FREE
by Nettie Farris

I'm thinking about adding Hank to the contacts in my phone. He messages me as much as anyone, so I'm thinking he deserves a real place in my life, even if it is just a line on a list. I'm wondering whether to enter him as *Hank* or *Frank*. Honestly, he is Hank, but I'd prefer he be *Frank,* his more ideal self. I'm thinking maybe if I see the solidity in him, he'll become more solid. Sort of what Michelangelo did with the Tuscan marble. Maybe I could enter him as both. Then his real self would be forced to battle his ideal self. The victor might be someone in between. Someone closer to the man I need.

BAD SEX
by MC DK

TRUE LOVE
by Valerie L. Wells

When we're old and gray
we'll sit on the porch and sway
on the swing
sit back and sing
old songs that we remember
and think back to that December
when we began life again
With one another
fresh and new
I'd have no other, no one else but you
you are my love and true
Knowing what's ahead, in store
is the biggest thrill;
this is no drill:
I can't wait to compare stories with you

* * *

by Zlatna Kostova

It's impossible, this love of ours:
I shouldn't be listening to your songs
all day
all night
I should not stay late
with my window open
for you to watch me

I know love blooms
in spring
but ours's just impossible—

I am a girl
you are a blackbird.

AFTER
by Jude McPherson

no one ever tells you about having
a broke(n) heart. cardiologist said i need to
rest. something that i've rarely done is
now the silver lining. if only i could smelt clouds
down to pay bills. maybe then i will. rent
this life a little longer.

AFTER PRIDE
by K. Nicole Wilson

I went to bed
with glitter
on half my body
shiny in red curls

in the morning
it's hardly there
on arm hairs
bare legs

and I imagine
it will never
completely leave
my bedsheets

some will remain
through washing
and drying cycles
and I wonder

(if I ever take
another lover)
if that surviving glitter
will cling to the one
who made me sing

so I won't have to

JUST BEFORE
by Whitney Baker

So now there is this black woman in my life,
after a winter of my reading my inbred Great Grandfather's
Civil War memoirs, thinking
"I have the mind to get into your shoes."

She is so black and so quiet,
African, Hutu or Tutsi,
I don't know, I haven't asked,
can't ask, literally,

and I won't ask the interpreter to ask for me.

Power falls forward in time
in its bloody exercise.

Its momentum is detail.

A piece of her ear
lands in the neighbor's mouth.

The whip slides between his legs
and its leather tip,
already bloody,
splits his cock about in half.

Who would know,
how would you know
how close to half?

How would you measure?

YESTERDAY
by Jordan Quinn

Dangling my feet from splintery beams,
it's kind of like it was yesterday
and you were there with your baseball cap cocked,
ready to bring the world to its knees
worshipping the essence of you:
shoulders blistered from too much sun,
shrugging with each side-step, cha-cha;
grin stretched too thin over not enough face,
leaving me wondering always
what could knock you flat on your back,
what could shatter that smile.

It's kind of like it was yesterday,
beams groaning, buckling
from too much girl on not enough boards,
but your ropy arms won't be there
when the splinters give way
to nothing but dusty air billowing silently
and the smell of how things were before.

TO THE GUY WHO ATE ALL MY SWEET POTATO CHIPS IN AL'S BAR ONE NIGHT
by Allison Thorpe

>After Alex Simand's "Poets at a Bar"

The last time I was in a bar
no one was eating
black bean burgers
among the clink of ice cubes
rolling empty in glasses.

No one was reading poetry
about awkward sex,
or sharing tears over
brotherly tributes,
or delving sacred wheels
and mysterious goddesses.

The last time I was in a bar
a man I didn't know
grabbed my ass
and huffed his smoky nothings
somewhere near my neck;
a friend, recently dumped,
threw up over her earth shoes,
the splatter tie dying
nearby bell bottoms;
a whiskey drenched cover band
slaughtered Grand Funk Railroad;
and my legs looked damn fine
in a leather fringed mini skirt.

So, thank you for telling me
about this place, this marvel
of night and poets,

and when I looked
where my sweet potato chips
had been and saw only
the crumb littered plate,
it seemed a fitting trade
for this nourishment
of new memories.

CRAIG'S LIST: MISSED CONNECTION
by Keith Stewart

I went under as soon as I saw you
standing in the glow of the dim streetlight.

I opened my mouth intending to speak
to you, but my voice, dark as a new moon

night, refused to shape even simple words
like "hello," "wait," "love," or "don't I know you?"

You cinched your coat belt tighter to your waist
as if you were chilled by my hungry stare

bearing its raw desire and loneliness
in effort to pierce into your marrow.

I began to believe you were my own
path to freedom, but without yet a word

spoken, you turned your back to me, waving
to another down the street, and left me.

THINGS WITH ME AND SPIDERS 2. NOCTURNE
by Bianca Bargo

The dark, for all the talk,
is not what terrifies.
It's the unseen—
or the not seeing—
and all the horrific
things you make of it.

You should see my
nightmares:

Usually everything
is made of snakes,
but often there's
a home invasion,
my teeth crumble
down to the gum,
or otherwise things
are just unnerving.

I have only dreamt of
spiders once:

An egg sac on the
ceiling unleashed a
stream of them,
dark and gleaming;
they spilled out
heavily in the
hundreds like
rice—cascading
down the walls
in sheets.

The clinking
sound of their
little brittle bodies
reminded me of
rain.

FOGGED
by Cleo

I walk in a fog
so thick the sand and sea
are obscure, interwoven,
any difference indiscernible.
I flow my steps into the cool
bay feeling seaweed
between my toes. I see
only clouds that engulf me
and my hand in front of my eyes.
I worry that my brain works in reverse,
it wanes like the outgoing tide.
I hope clarity emerges
through the steamy mist
that covers my world.

BEING ALONE
by Amanda Holt

Some days it feels like
The copy of "Great Expectations" forgotten,
Half-read, in the seat-back pocket of the plane
to China.
Or, like the last forward
Reflex of a smooshed spider leg.

But today,
Today, it feels like the moonbow
When the clouds part,
cutting the mist of Cumberland Falls,
painting it with dim but enduring
light.

RUNNING
by Abigail Caldwell-Gatsos

I'm running
Constantly running
From then till now I've been in limbo
Escaping
Trying to get away from feeling anything
I watched you
From the moment I was born
I learned from you
Now I'm just running
From him
From everything
Constantly running
Trying to push away
Trying to forget
Why is it all catching up to me now
Why am I reliving it now
Watching you
Slip away
Not slip
Violently yanked
Torn from this world of being
I'm running
Constantly running

GEORGIA AQUARIUM BELUGA WHALE CALF DIES
by Leigh Anne Hornfeldt

Still, as an unrung bell her heart
stopped just after 7 a.m. Her body hoisted
from the water's palm, leather
straps straining against dead
weight. The exhibit has closed. They say
it will reopen when it is deemed in the best interest

of the animals. Unlike humans,
whales are conscious breathers—even when sleeping
they must remember
in & out.
In stillness they know.
These bodies were never
ours to begin with.

WHAT I'LL WRITE ABOUT IF I EVER WRITE A POEM ABOUT MY WIFE

by Jason Williams

A handclasp beneath my pillow
desperate,
metacarpals twisting in her grip.

The tumor leaned in
all seven centimeters of him
slicing the edge of his fingernails into flesh
tearing my kidney away in strips.

Curled toes,
tangled legs,
arched back,
flinging blankets from the bed
gasping
"Please God, please God."
gasping.

But still the handclasp
and across two feet of pillows
shimmering eyes
steadily staring into my twisted face.

No words.
But I heard these:
I will not let you go.

FACING IT
by Nora Burton

Cleaning out my drawer, making
room for the new by
clearing out the old I found your
wallet, the black one that you
always carried, the one the nurse
handed me just after the doctor
said, "we called it." Lost then I placed
it in my drawer
under my jeans for safekeeping.
Now I grasp the black leather
and spread it apart to see: your driver's
license, your bank card, credit cards,
pictures of the kids, a receipt from the
gas station when you last stopped to fill
the car. Closing the wallet I place
it back in the drawer under my jeans
and leave a room that has suddenly
grown cold.

SEVEN CIRCLES
by Sue Churchill

The priest on NPR
called his terminal diagnosis
the best thing that ever happened to him.
My brain was on airplane mode,
slipping into hibernation.
That kind of talk.
Cheery hospice propaganda,
easy to avow in a radio interview
with your leukemia in remission,
before the steroids, before the final
failed marrow transplants.

But he said something more,
something from a long haul
working with street gangs
that pulled me back, set me spinning:
"Death is a punk. So many worse things
put death in its place–make a list!
You'll see what I mean."
And, I have, and it's true.

The list is an endless descent
that spirals back, a Mobius strip.
You end up where you started,
but it's not the same.
Where the descent takes you, no one
wants to go. But, after you go there,
anywhere else is *Up*.

Try it. Start with the same diagnosis
for your child or lover. You immortal.

Envision different fates,
airplane crashes, tsunamis, death alone
in the street, an addict, by murder,
the indifferent or aroused eyes of your killer.

This happening to your child or lover.
It gets graphic.

Let's skip for now the gruesome
TV scenarios, but if you're having
trouble, tune in, any channel.

Vary the theme. Someone you love,
some awful death, but your fault—
you ran the fatal stop sign, drunk.

For a deeper twist, imagine
the flip side, intent.
You're the killer. Alive alright,
your own empty eyes in the mirror.
Or your grown child, the pedophile.
Wake up to that pure grain despair.

And, still, this is the easy stuff.
Try imaging the world without trees,
no shade, no twigs, no leaves fluttering.
Or, without birds, nothing alive in the sky,
no sudden bit of song, no wings.
Without rain, an eternal drought
 cracked and brown, only salt
where there was strand—the beginning
of the end of the planet. The real deal.
For everybody, not just you.

Now come back to you, ill, in a clean bed
with pain pills, people to care for you
not a hero, but not without honor
one headstone later, on a rainy day.
It's alright.

THE POETS

Mary L. Allen, a resident of Lexington, writes poetry, essays and book reviews and reads extensively in several genres. She is a founding member of Bluegrass Wordsmiths.

Bobby Steve Baker lives in Lexington, Kentucky having grown up on the Canadian side of Lake Huron. He has two Chapbooks of poetry, *Numbered Bones* from Accents Publishing chapbook contest and *The Taste of Summer Lightning* from Finishing Line Press. His first full length book of poetry, with original ekphrastic photography and art is *This Crazy Urge To Live* by Linnet's Wings Press.

Whitney Baker

Eduardo Ballestero was born in San Carlos, Costa Rica and grew up in Kentucky. He has a BA in English from the University of Kentucky and lives and works in Lexington. He is at work on a collection of persona poems.

Bianca Bargo is an Appalachian whose interests are numerous and sundry. Winner of the 2009 University of Kentucky's Farquhar Poetry Award, her work has appeared in *Limestone: A Journal of Art and Literature*, and *Bigger than they Appear: Anthology of Very Short Poems*. She is the author of the chapbook *How I Became an Angry Woman* (Accents Publishing, 2015).

Jennifer Barricklow is a writer and freelance editor in Lexington Kentucky. In addition to poetry, she also enjoys tarot, gardening, and making stuff out of yarn. She attends meetings of local writers' groups and occasionally leads writing workshops.

Elizabeth Beck is a writer, teacher and artist. She is the author of two books of poetry. In 2011, she founded The Teen Howl Poetry Series that serves the youth of central Kentucky.

Jennifer Beckett graduated from Georgetown College with a Bachelor of Arts in English. She earned her Master of Arts in English at the University of Kentucky. She teaches high school English and French. Spending time with her family brings her joy.

Gaby Bedetti is a long time professor in the English Department at EKU.

Hannah Bishop became a writer at the Kentucky Center Governor's School for the Arts. Ever since then, she has been writing because she can't seem to stop.

Don Boes was born in Louisville, Kentucky. His collections of poetry include *The Eighth Continent* (Northeastern University Press) and *Railroad Crossing* (Finishing Line Press). His newest book is *Good Luck With That* (FutureCycle Press). He teaches at Bluegrass Community and Technical College.

Dorothy Bouzouma is a writer currently living in Lexington, Kentucky. These days she mainly dabbles in Creative Nonfiction, but poetry was one of her first true loves. In 2013 she placed as 2nd runner-up in the Ploughshares Emerging Writers Contest. Her most recent essay, "Zahna," was published in March 2015 in *Slice Literary Magazine*. She doesn't believe in genre-rules. In the end, it's all just poetry.

Colin Boyd

Maggie Brewer is a history teacher originally from Ohio. She has now lived in Kentucky for almost half of her life and although she still finds some aspects new and surreal, it is home.

Terre Brothers Johnson: Mother, Writer, Seeker.

Kari Burchfield

Joan Burke is an occasional poet and a writer documenting the cancer journey of her beloved husband. She is improving a rock garden, and loves yoga & dancing. Also, sometimes, she is Joan Babbage Burke: Cat Nurse.

A senior at Transylvania University, **Elizabeth Burton** has had work published in the *Yeah Write!*, *Writer's Review*, the *Albion Review*, various independent zines, and the 2014 Lexington Poetry Month anthology. There are few things in this world she loves as much as Lexington, but if she had to pick, she would say strongly-brewed iced tea, Ale-8-One, road trips, and Sailor Moon.

Nora Burton holds and MFA in Creative Writing from Murray State University. She teaches English at Eastern Kentucky University and is the author of two memoirs and numerous poems and essays.

Linda Caldwell is a poet and playwright writing in Paint Lick, Kentucky.

Abigail Caldwell-Gatsos is an aspiring writer and poet and has been writing since before she knew how to spell. In her writing, her aim is to make a mark in the world and to show people their not alone in the constant struggle through life's challenges.

Robert Campbell is a poet living in Lexington, Kentucky. Robert holds an MS in Library Science from the University of Kentucky and is currently an MFA student in poetry at Murray State University. He serves as Reference & Instruction Librarian at Transylvania University and Reviews Editor at *DIALOGIST*, an online journal of poetry and art.

Amy Camuglia considers herself a "folk poet". Her poetry flies into one of her many journals and lands on a solid branch, rarely edited. Unpolished, and from the heart, her eclectic collection of written work includes everything from pain-filled prose to comedy relief, bird-watching to freestyle rap.

Joseph Camuglia is a singer/songwriter, who traverses the country as a wandering troubadour. A melodic bard, who, on many occasions has earned a nice meal by singing his poetic anthems.

Brittany Castle

Karlee Caswell is a rising junior. She attends Lafayette Senior High School and has been a member of the SCAPA Literary Arts program since the fourth grade.

Erin Chandler is an author, playwright, actress and producer from Versailles, Kentucky. She currently resides in North Carolina and is working on an MFA in Creative Non-Fiction from Spalding University.

Sherry Chandler's latest book, *The Woodcarver's Wife*, has been described as "quaint but smoldering." Look for her work in the *Louisville Review*, *Kestrel*, and *Calyx*.

Lucia Cherciu is a Professor of English at SUNY / Dutchess in Poughkeepsie, NY, and she writes both in English and in Romanian. Her newest book of poetry, *Edible Flowers*, was published by Main Street Rag in February 2015.

Sue Churchill is a writer, former teacher, and manager of Thistles End Farm, where she lives in a high bend of the Kentucky River.

Chuck Clenney, a Covington-native, resides in the northside of beautiful Lexington, Kentucky. By day, a Japanese translator, and, all other times, is a visual artist, poet, radio DJ, event planner, and word nerd. He is the current Hip Hop Director at WRFL 88.1FM and does a radio show every Tuesday night from 10–Midnight.

Rae Cobbs is a poet and writer who has been twice honored by grants from the Kentucky Foundation for Women, first for working on *Leaky Boat*, her manuscript of poetry, and in 2013 for writing *Blake's Crossing*, a novel in progress. She lives in Louisville, writing and typing/editing others' work.

Debbie Adams Cooper is a native Appalachian now living in central Kentucky.

Sean L Corbin is an MFA candidate in Creative Writing at the University of Kentucky. His work has been featured in quite a few places. He teaches composition and speech at UK. Sean lives in Lexington with his wife, the writer Amanda Kelley, and their children.

Tara Cremeans-Mounger: still searching for something worth writing about herself.

Heather Dent is a freelance illustrator and part-time library page at the Champaign Public Library. She writes children's books, poetry, personal essays, and occasionally short stories. She got her BA in sociology at Berea College and now lives with her husband and 4 year old son in Champaign, Illinois.

Andrew Depew wants to be on track to be a teacher by the time these lines reach ink.

Serena Devi is in the SCAPA Literary Arts program at Lafayette High School. She dyes her hair a lot and watches too much reality TV.

Bernie Deville is an MFA student in Creative Writing at EKU and teaches at Providence Montessori Middle School.

Julian DeVille is an honors math major at EKU, who has been writing on the side since high school. His work mostly focuses on the potential and odd nature of the human mind, but recently he has been attempting to create poems which follow algebraic structures he has studied, to make poems that break the left to right top to bottom order in which poems normally read.

Laurel Dixon lives in Lexington, Kentucky. She won first place in The Carnegie Center's LGBT Writing Contest for her story "How to Fall in

Love with Straight Girls," and her poetry has been published in *Tobacco Magazine, Words Dance Magazine, Voicemail Poems* and *The Legendary*. She spends most of her time writing, gardening, and drinking too much coffee.

MC DK was accused of kidnapping royalty by a plumber with a mushroom addiction. Since his acquittal, DK has been expressing his outrage through poetry.

Mary Dusing is a Kentucky girl who shuns shoes and is most at home where things are sultry and slow-moving. You can find her by day happily sauntering about with test tubes and mice, smiling like a circus clown (only way less creepy) and by evening plinking away at a keyboard trying to keep up with her wayward thoughts.

M J Eaton was the first female Poet-in-the-Schools in Kentucky, and went on to be awarded 13 more grants from the National Endowment to be Poet-in-the-Schools in Tennessee, Missouri, Arkansas, and Iowa. She has published with Scholastic Publications and August House. She presently lives in Missouri, where she is working on her next book of poems.

Lynnell Edwards is the author of three full length collections of poetry, most recently *Covet* (2011) and a chapbook, *Kings of the Rock and Roll Hotshop* (Accents, 2014). She now lives in Louisville, where she is on the faculty at Spalding University, though she attended Henry Clay High School and is a proud graduate of Maxwell Elementary, and Morton Jr. High!

HB Elam is. At some point in the future he will not be. He is certain about that, and everything else he is not certain about. Get to know him while you can.

Poetessa Leixyl Kaye Emmerson is a Friday's child that was born in the Year of the Fire Horse. Her childhood was spent living in many different areas of the North Eastern, Southern and Mid-Western parts of the U.S. She has been writing stories and poetry since she was 4 years old. Leixyl was a 2014 Pushcart Nominee. She lists motherhood as her biggest accomplishment.

Stevie Farmer

Nettie Farris is the author of *Communion* (Accents Publishing, 2013) and *Fat Crayons* (Finishing Line Press, 2015).

K. Bruce Florence works as a college administrator and is married and has two grown children. His publishing experiences are primarily in anthologies and journals. He has a novel in progress, but enjoys writing poetry more.

Katrin Flores attends Lafayette High School. She likes to binge-watch documentaries on Netflix whenever possible.

Chloe G. Forsting graduated from Berea College in May of 2015 with an English major and a reconstructed sense of self. She was born and lives in Louisville, Kentucky. She is a Capricorn.

Sarah Freligh is the author of *A Brief Natural History of an American Girl*, winner of the Editor's Choice award from Accents Publishing, and *Sort of Gone*, a book of poems that follows the rise and fall of a fictional pitcher named Al Stepansky. *Sad Math*, the winner of the Moon City Poetry Award, is forthcoming in November 2015.

Duke Gatsos started writing poetry in high school and continued into college. He had the good fortune to attend workshops at UK under the direction of Jane Vance and some talented writers. The solid poetry community in Lexington keeps him writing.

Michayla Gatsos

Karen George, author of *Into the Heartland, Inner Passage, Swim Your Way Back, Seed of Me*, and forthcoming *The Fire Circle*, has work in *Memoir, Louisville Review, Naugatuck River Review*, and *Still*. She reviews poetry at Poetry Matters, and is fiction editor of the journal *Waypoints*. Her website is: *karenlgeorge.snack.ws*.

Pauletta Hansel is a writer, teacher and author of five poetry collections, most recently *The Lives We Live in Houses* (Wind Publications, 2011) and *What I Did There* (Dos Madres Press, 2011) and *Tangle*, out soon. She is co-editor of *Pine Mountain Sand & Gravel*, the literary publication of Southern Appalachian Writers Cooperative.

Matthew Haughton is the author of two collections of poems, *Stand in the Stillness of Woods* and *Bee-coursing Box*.

Jeffrey Helton is a native of Western North Carolina and an alumnus of Berea College, where he studied English and Philosophy. He's currently transitioning out of an AmeriCorps VISTA position with

Grow Appalachia. Jeffrey is the founder and editor of *Pollen,* an online literary magazine dedicated to the relationship between folks and food in Appalachia.

An English Teacher from Lexington, Kentucky, **Amanda Holt** has written poetry since she could read Shel Silverstein. Toward the end of her studies at Transylvania University, she decided to tattoo the last full sentence of her favorite poem ("In Blackwater Woods") on her back, and has been spreading poetry to unsuspecting questioners ever since.

Kristy Robinson Horine is a Kentucky writer: journalist by trade, creative by heart. She makes her life in Paris with her husband, Eric, and four children—Hanson, Anna, Emy, and Sadie. Her professional and creative work has been published in newspapers, magazines and anthologies in Kentucky and Southern Indiana.

Leigh Anne Hornfeldt is the author of *The Intimacy Archive* and the editor of Two of Cups Press.

Hap Houlihan is a Lexington native and co-founder of LexPoMo. He's the general manager of Lexington Community Radio, and encourages you to listen and contribute (content, time, or even money) to our station. He lives nearby with his woman, children, and animals.

Alx Johns is an Associate Professor of English at the University of North Georgia, where he teaches creative writing and American literature. He was born and raised in Atlanta, Georgia and currently reside in the Athens, Georgia area.

Jiv Johnson is a writer from Mount Sterling, Kentucky. He mainly writes poetry about mundane and not-mundane events that happen around him in Kentucky. He has a mother, a father, and a brother.

Carole Johnston is still obsessed with Japanese short form poetry. She still drives around the Eastern third of the U.S. with her notebook and camera, capturing those "aha" moments. Her chapbook, *Journeys: Getting Lost* is available from Finishing Line Press or Amazon.com.

Amanda Kelley has worked as a graduate assistant, advertising sales representative, substitute teacher, newspaper reporter, delivery driver, property manager, and retail salesperson at a hardware store and at a lingerie shop. She is currently an MFA candidate in the Creative Writing Program at UK.

Robert S. King, a native Georgian, now lives in Lexington, Kentucky. His poems have appeared in hundreds of magazines. He has published eight collections of poetry, most recently *Diary of the Last Person on Earth* (Sybaritic Press, 2014) and *Developing a Photograph of God* (Glass Lyre Press, 2014).

c.l. kirby: Social worker. Therapist. Peace Corps Volunteer.

Michelle Knickerbocker is a quirky poet and cook who lives in Frankfort, Kentucky with her wife, cats, dog, and axolotl. She daydreams about napping in the sunshine, dragons, and cooking in roomy kitchens with well honed knives and endless ingredients.

Bulgarian-born translator, journalist, radio-host and poetess **Zlatna Kostova** graduated in English and American literature from Sofia University, Bulgaria. She has one poetry book (*Sparrow in a Nutshell,* 2012) and another pending. She has translated many plays, films, poems, short stories and books. She also writes song lyrics in English and Bulgarian.

Jonathon La Mar lives in Kentucky.

Jim Lally sleeps in the breeze under the stars, avoids ceiling fans and like-minded poets, can't stay out of "falling rock" zones.

Jude Lally writes and recites poetry as an outlet for his creative needs and as a means of enlightening, inspiring, engaging and entertaining listeners. Jude is a member of the poetry group Poezia, occasionally attends The Poet's Supper and the Artcroft writer's group outside of Carlisle, Kentucky, and is a regular presenter at the Holler Poets series events.

JD Lester writes—and promptly misplaces—poems on an irregular basis, causing her to wonder if she should try to one day rustle them up and - oh, look! A flower!

Lennart Lundh is a poet, short-fictionist, historian, and photographer. His work has appeared internationally since 1965. Len and his wife, Lin, reside in northeastern Illinois.

George Ella Lyon's most recent collections are *Many-Storied House* and *Voice from the March on Washington* (co-written with J. Patrick Lewis). She is Kentucky's current Poet Laureate.

Patrick Maloney is a semi-professional procrastinator, a sit-down tragic, and a self-proclaimed overall sit-down guy. When he isn't staring off into space, he finds the time to rhyme about the crooks in his crooked mind.

Allie Marini (Batts) holds degrees from Antioch University of Los Angeles & New College of Florida, meaning she can explain deconstructionism, but cannot perform simple math. She is managing editor for the *NonBinary Review, Unbound Octavo,* & Zoetic Press, and co-edits for Lucky Bastard Press with her man, performance poet B Deep.

Erin Mathews is a Lexington native and second-year English Literature and Art History Major at the University of Cincinnati. She writes for herself, family, and friends.

Jay McCoy spends his days selling books and leading writing workshops. He just completed his MFA from the Bluegrass Writers Studio. Jay has published his work in several journals and anthologies. His first book, *The Occuption,* was published in 2015.

Christopher McCurry teaches high school English and is an editor at Accents Publishing. He is a Kentucky Teacher Fellow at the Bread Loaf School of English and the author of *Splayed,* a chapbook of love poems.

Jude McPherson is just bobbin n weavin.

Christopher Miller is a Yankee who migrated to the Lexington area in 2004. He is a practicing Buddhist who enjoys heavy metal music, reading, meditation, playing guitar, losing at tennis, and watching the birds at his feeders. He lives in Jessamine County, Kentucky with his cat and two dogs.

Jason Lee Miller, MFA, is a communications professional in Berea, Kentucky. His poetry, fiction, essays, and book reviews have appeared in *94 Creations, Blood Lotus, Bluegrass Accolade, The Copperfield Review, Crack the Spine* and more. His debut, full-length poetry collection is due out late 2015.

Madison Miller is a college student in Lexington, Kentucky. Madison's current lifestyle consists of 94 hour work weeks, way too much caffeine, zoloft, and whatever else life throws her way.

Joshua Aaron Moore is a Lovely, Kentucky native who loves basketball, "Power Rangers," and country music. He graduated from the University of Kentucky in 2013 with a double major in Integrated Strategic Communication and English. His first two e-books, *Dark Peace* and *No Fries,* are available on Amazon.

JW Mullins is a husband, father of twins. His wife and he own and operate Nina & Wes Photography. He graduated from University of

South Carolina with a BA in English Literature in '09. In 2014 he received a Certificate of Christian Apologetics from Biola University.

Sue Neufarth Howard: Poet and visual artist, member—Greater Cincinnati Writers League (GCWL) and Colerain Artists. Received Third Prize and/or Honorable Mention in several Ohio Poetry Day Contests since 1998.

Joseph Allen Nichols lives in Lexington, Kentucky with his two sons, Isaac and Jonathan. He writes poetry, short stories, nonfiction, and, since his schoolin' is days from complete, will soon return to his half-finished novel. This is his second year participating in LexPoMo.

Bronson O'Quinn is a writer from Lexington, Kentucky.

Pat Owen divides her time between Louisville and Sarasota. She's been published in *The Louisville Review* and *This Wretched Vessel* and is the author of *Crossing the Sky Bridge,* by Larkspur Press. She studied in the Spalding MFA program and has been a long-time member of the writing group, Chartreuse Table.

Ashley Parker Owens is the owner of the indie press KY Story, proud publisher of thirteen anthologies celebrating the Kentucky, Appalachian, and Southern voice. Her work has recently appeared in *Hogglepot, Rose Red, Egg Poetry, Boston Poetry Magazine, Quail Bell, Imaginarium,* and *Tinderbox Magazine.* Reach her at parker.owens@gmail.com or kystory.net.

Jeremy Paden is an Associate Professor of Spanish and Latin American at Transylvania University in Lexington, Kentucky. His poems and translations have appeared in various journals and anthologies. He is the author of *Broken Tulips,* a chapbook of poems.

Rayny Palmer is alive.

Tina Parker grew up in Bristol, Virginia, and now lives in Berea, Kentucky, with her husband and two young daughters. Her full-length poetry collection *Mother May I* was published by Sibling Rivalry Press in 2016.

Maya Pemble is a seventh grade girl who attends Providence Montessori Middle School. She currently lives in Sadieville, Kentucky with her parents, sister, dog, and two snails. Her many hobbies include ballet, piano, horseback riding, writing, cooking, swimming, making bad puns, and climbing trees. She is ecstatic to be a part of LexPoMo this year.

LaTosha Pence is a Missouri native poet born in '91. She has been published 4 times, including at BCTC in Lexington, Kentucky, the "B-section" newspaper in Berea, Kentucky, *Salvation.org* online, and in a novel called *Stars of our Hearts*. She has created two groups: "Poetry Pod" and "Poet Tree" on Facebook.

Catherine Perkins, aka **Cleo**, born a Navy brat at Fort Ord, California in 1955, has been writing since she was a teen. It wasn't until after moving from the farm (2004) in Paris, Kentucky to the big city, Lexington and being introduced to The Carnegie Center for Literacy and Learning did her desire to become a good poet and writer awaken in her.

B. David Perry: A 1975 University of Kentucky graduate and native Lexingtonian with a reverence for the written word as it was taught. Retired Division of Abandoned Mine Lands, 2008, still seeking "the healing power of landscape" through stream fishing in the Appalachians.

Liz Prather teaches writing at SCAPA-Lafayette.

Dennis J. Preston is a native Kentuckian living in Owensboro. Retired from teaching, he is pastor of The Mt. Zion Cumberland Presbyterian Church. He received his doctorate from Louisville Presbyterian Theological Seminary, and enjoys reading, writing, traveling, and spending time with his family. His first book of poetry is *In the Ash Heap: Poems From the Book of Job*.

Melva Sue Priddy has been talking to herself or writing, or ... well ... both, since she can remember. In addition to writing, she loves writing friends, gardening, grandmamaing & studying.

Most of **Jordan Quinn**'s inspiration comes from her tendency to be a night owl, her fluency in Spanglish, and the utter divinity that is dark chocolate. She has lived in Lexington for the past six years, and after much deliberation and time spent pouring poems solely into her laptop, has finally mustered up the courage to join Lexington Poetry Month.

Delmar Reffett is a PhD student in English Literature at the University of Kentucky. When not buried to his elbows in British Modernism, he enjoys writing poetry and short fiction of his own.

Rona Roberts hosts Savoring Kentucky, one of Kentucky's longest-running food blogs. Rona speaks and writes about the pleasures of Kentucky food and champions those who produce it. She is the author of

Sweet, Sweet Sorghum: Kentucky's Golden Wonder and *Classic Kentucky Meals: Stories, Ingredients and Recipes from the Traditional Bluegrass Kitchen.*

Barbara Sabol is a speech therapist and teacher. She is a graduate of Spalding University's MFA program. Barbara has published two chapbooks, *Original Ruse* and *The Distance Between Blues,* and her poetry has appeared in several anthologies and numerous journals. She also publishes poetry book reviews/interviews in the blog, Poetry Matters.

After more than four decades of teaching, **Jonel Sallee** is discovering the joys of the "retired life," and finds that, like Stephen Daedalus, she has grown "weary of ardent ways." Thus, she is seeking to celebrate other possible ways of being.

A native of central Pennsylvania, **Elizabeth Sands Wise** now calls central Kentucky home. She lives and writes from within the chaotic world of toddler children.

Douglas E. Self is whatever you think.

Sandra Sofiah Sexton is a resident of her home state of Kentucky. She holds a BS in Elementary Education from University of Cincinnati, a MSLS in Library and Information Science from University of Kentucky, and a MS in Psychology from University of Phoenix. Mother of two sons who both graduated from the US Naval Academy. Grandmother of seven.

Alex Simand tells himself he is a writer daily, though he works full time as an engineer in San Francisco. He is currently working on his MFA in Creative Writing from Antioch University Los Angeles. Alex writes about love, hate, cultural otherness, and fantasies between strangers.

Vijay Singh is a dreamer-poet in his leisure hours and a research scientist in professional work. At present, he is Robinson Chair Professor of Electrical and Computer Engineering at University of Kentucky, Lexington. Vijay did his Ph.D. work at University of Minnesota, where he met his artist wife, Carolyn, *laudablemudstudio.com.*

Savannah Sipple is a writer from eastern Kentucky. Her work has been published in *Appalachian Heritage, The Pikeville Review, Southern Indiana Review, Still: The Journal, Now & Then, Deep South Magazine, The Louisville Review,* and *New Southerner.*

Misty Skaggs, 34, is a poet, short story author and two-time college dropout. She currently resides on her Mamaw's couch way out at the end of

Beartown Ridge Road where she is slowly amassing a massive second-hand library and perfecting her buttermilk biscuits. Her work primarily concerns the people and culture of modern Appalachia.

GA Smith enjoys bourbon with Ale81, or in an old-fashioned. His yelps are notorious for echoing against the walls of Al's Bar during Holler. Noted for use of suspenders and shirts with a minimum of three buttons open; his work has been featured in *The Lumbaryard, pluck!,* and others.

Meadow Smith: female, 5/7, dirty blonde hair, blue eyes.

Affrilachian Poet and Cave Canem Fellow, **Bianca Lynne Spriggs** is an award-winning poet and multidisciplinary artist from Lexington, Kentucky. Bianca is the author the forthcoming titles, *Call Her By Her Name* (Northwestern University Press, 2016) and *The Galaxy is a Dance Floor* (Argos Books, 2016), as well as co-editor of *Circe's Lament: An Anthology of Wild Women Poetry* (Accents Publishing, 2015).

Jennifer Standard is the single mother of two boys, born & raised in Louisville.

Keith Stewart is a writer and poet from Hyden, Kentucky. This is his third year participating in LexPoMo.

Karah Stokes gardens, teaches, and writes in the heart of the Kentucky Bluegrass.

Katerina Stoykova-Klemer is the author of several poetry books in English and Bulgarian, most recently *The Porcupine of Mind* (Broadstone Books, 2012, in English) and *How God Punishes* (ICU, 2014, in Bulgarian), which won the Ivan Nikolov National Poetry Prize.

Victoria Sullivan is a second-year MA student at the University of Kentucky, pursuing a degree in Literature. Born and raised in Eastern Kentucky, she takes great pride in her roots and hopes to use her work in critique and creative writing to glorify the region.

Jessica Swafford was challenged to Lexington Poetry Month 2015 by her friend and sister-in-law, Crystal Bruin, as a means to fight and cope with Jessica's battle with uterine cancer. Crystal, never having written a poem before, took the challenge right along side Jessica.

Jessica Taylor is an avid writer who currently studies at Transylvania University in downtown Lexington. She is editor-in-chief of the school's literary magazine, *The Transylvanian*. While she studies communication, in hopes to strengthen her poetry skills on the side, you can find her popping into local readings, such as Teen Howl and Holler.

Rudy Thomas: Poet, editor, publisher with works in anthologies, literary journals statewide and international ... A speaker for the Kentucky Arts Council Speakers' Bureau ... Author of 29 books ... Educator and Lindsey Wilson College Upward Bound Director ...

Allison Thorpe is the author of *Thoughts While Swinging a Wild Child in a Green Mesh Hammock* (Janze Publications), *Swooning and Other Art Forms* (a NFSPS chapbook winner), *What She Sees: Poems for Georgia O'Keefe* (forthcoming in June digitally from White Knuckle Press), and *Dorothy's Glasses* (forthcoming from Finishing Line Press).

A sophomore at Woodford County High School, **Alexis Tipton** continues to write poetry and takes creative writing classes.

Beatrice Underwood-Sweet is a wandering poet, now living in her fourth state as an adult. Her work has been published in *The Sun Magazine, Aurora, Her Limestone Bones,* and *This Wretched Vessel.*

Kendrick VanZant works as an analyst. He is currently writing music and libretto for a musical drama.

Randall Walden. 27. The new American poet. No accomplishments to mention.

Luke Wallin has eight award-winning books for children and young adults, as well as books on writing about nature and culture, and, with Eva Gordon, on writing for children. Luke holds an MFA from the Iowa Writer's Workshop, and is Emeritus Professor of English at the University of Massachusetts Dartmouth; he taught for many years in Spalding University's MFA in Creative Writing.

Valerie L Wells is a former Lexingtonian, who resides out in New Mexico. Pushing the boundaries of photography, art, and working on the written word the older I become. Trying to encompass all of these things into a symbiotic relationship.

Originally from Catlettsburg, Kentucky, **Jason Williams** works as a software developer in Lexington. His work has been published in *Appalachian Quarterly, Kudzu,* and a few other places.

K. Nicole Wilson is a Limestone (AKA Maysville) native and is finally beginning to feel home again after living out West for nearly a decade.

She strives for the equality of quality on the page as well as with a microphone, and is known here and there as the Sports Poet.

Harriet Windsor writes poetry, fiction, and creative non-fiction. In 2010, she received a grant from the Kentucky Foundation to work on two novels: *Ms. Faust* and *Both Sides Now (or, The Ideology of Love)*. She has published short fiction and poetry in a number of print and online publications.

J. Wise: Teacher, aka the great American hustler: pedagogical Butch Cassidy, literary Sundance Kid; walking thesaurus/dictionary; critical reader; bad dancer; dreamer of impossible dreams.

Elle Wong

Holly Wooten is a high school English teacher, blogger, dog lover, optimist, and seeker of all things lovely.

T.D. Worthington: a dude. a lover of *X-files* and all things humor, a student journalist, cartoonist, and a busy dude it seems like. Lately he's been doing what he loves and lovin' what he does. Featured in *Her Limestone Bones* and *This Wretched Vessel* and the WRFL-zine *RiFLe*.

Aidan Ziliak is an unpaid student of Liz Prather and Christopher McCurry. Lafayette class of '15.

ABOUT THE EDITOR

A Pushcart Prize nominee, Christopher McCurry's poems have appeared in *Diode, Limestone, Louisville Review, Rabbit Catastrophe Review,* the *LA Review, Rattle* and others. In 2013 he came in second place in the Robert Haiduke poetry contest and won *Still: the Journal*'s fiction contest judged by Holly Goddard Jones. His second chapbook *Nearly Perfect Photograph* is currently available from Two of Cups Press. As a high school English teacher, Christopher receives a generous fellowship from the C.E. & S. foundation to attend the Bread Loaf School of English. Christopher currently lives in Lexington, Kentucky with his wife, Eloise, and his daughter, Abra. In 2015, he co-founded Workhorse, a literary collective for writers.

SPONSORS

We would like to express our heartfelt gratitude to the following organizations and businesses who made this project possible:

www.ingramcontent.com/pod-product-compliance
Lightning Source LLC
Chambersburg PA
CBHW021435080526
44588CB00009B/533